SECRET
OTTAWA

SECRET OTTAWA

The Unique Guidebook to Ottawa's Hidden Sites, Sounds, & Tastes

Laura Byrne Paquet

WITH PHOTOGRAPHS BY
Linda Rutenberg

ECW PRESS

The publication of *Secret Ottawa* has been generously supported by the Canada Council, the Ontario Arts Council, and the Government of Canada through the Book Publishing Industry Development Program.

CANADIAN CATALOGUING IN PUBLICATION DATA

Paquet, Laura Byrne, 1965-
Secret Ottawa: the unique guidebook to
Ottawa's hidden sites, sounds, & tastes
ISBN 1-55022-435-2
1. Ottawa (Ont.) – Guidebooks. I. Title.
FC3096.18.P36 2000 917.13'84044 C00-931713-9
F1059.5.O9P36 2000

Original series design by Paul Davies, ECW Type and Art, Oakville, Ontario.
Typesetting by Martel *en-tête*.
Imaging and cover by Guylaine Régimbald – SOLO DESIGN.
Printed by Printcrafters Inc., Winnipeg, Manitoba, Canada.

Distributed in Canada by General Distribution Services,
325 Humber College Blvd., Etobicoke, Ontario M9W 7C3.

Distributed in the United States by LPC Group,
1436 West Randolph Street, Chicago, Illinois, U.S.A. 60607.

Published by ECW PRESS,
2120 Queen Street East, Suite 200, Toronto, Ontario M4E 1E2.

www.ecwpress.com

PRINTED AND BOUND IN CANADA

TABLE OF CONTENTS

SECRET . . .

INTRODUCTION

When I first approached Robert Lecker at ECW Press with the idea of writing a book in his Secret Guides series called *Secret Ottawa*, he was interested but cautious. "Are there enough secrets in *Ottawa* to make a book?" he asked with all the scepticism of the true Montrealer.

"Of course," I bristled, rising to my adopted city's defence, as I have done so many times before. Yet, as always, I understood the scepticism.

Ottawa is an easy city to underestimate, to pigeonhole, to dismiss. The phrase "government town" sums up a whole zeitgeist in two words: a place where the people are conservative, where the bureaucracy strangles true city life, and where the fun never starts. True, the city has had its boring days (my sister, who went to school in Ottawa in the mid-1970s, couldn't get out fast enough). But it certainly has enough secrets to fill a book.

It's no longer just a government town. Sure, office complexes all over Ottawa still hum with the sound of white-collar people pushing paper around. But in early 2000, high technology overtook government as the region's number-one employer. The place is rolling in dot.com cash.

As I explored the region on both sides of the Ottawa River doing research for this book, what struck me time and again is how much this city is evolving. Neighbourhoods that seemed sleepy and moribund just a couple of years ago are now thrumming with life. Local volunteer groups are starting up new sports leagues and theatre troupes with endless energy. Ten years ago, you'd have been hard-pressed to get a decent burger in Ottawa after midnight. Now you can dance to alternative music, shop for a power saw, bet at the track, or work out at the gym until six the next morning.

Time after time when I told friends, neighbours, and total strangers about this book, their first reaction was "Well, if I tell you about my favourite secret, it's not going to be a secret anymore, is it?" Maybe that's why Ottawa has had such a staid reputation for so many years: the locals have been keeping all the good news to themselves.

Well, sorry folks, I'm blowing your cover. I hope that *Secret Ottawa* helps the rest of you to discover the hidden corners and offbeat places of the nation's capital, beyond the indisputable treasures of Parliament Hill, the national museums, and the major historic sites. And I hope that you revel in this compact, quirky, ever-changing region as much as I do.

HOW TO USE
SECRET OTTAWA

The entries in this book are arranged in alphabetical order by subject, so whether your interest is architecture, Elvis, gardening, or wine, you can find it quickly. Two things that I haven't supplied, in most cases, are hours of operation and directions. The first change about as frequently as Madonna's accent, and the second should be self-evident in most cases (and, when they're not, it's probably best to phone the information number for detailed instructions on how to get to the place from your location).

All telephone numbers are in the 613 area code unless otherwise noted (in a few cases, where 613 is included, the phone number is a long-distance call from downtown Ottawa). Note that many places in the 819 area code — such as Hull, Aylmer, Gatineau, and numerous villages — are local calls from downtown Ottawa. So, try dialling the number without the area code first and see what happens.

Speaking of dialling, here's a word to the wise: nothing changes faster than the retail and restaurant businesses. Unfortunately, a great store or a cool restaurant that I've visited and raved about today will have disappeared without a trace tomorrow. So do call first.

Of course, the daily, weekly, and even monthly media will be much more current than any book. For movie listings, concert information, and the latest scoop on the Ottawa entertainment scene, pick up a copy of *Ottawa X Press*, available free at many downtown bars and restaurants. For gay and lesbian news, there's *Capital Xtra*, also widely distributed. *Tone*, available in health-food stores and other alternative businesses, provides the scoop on everything from aromatherapy to Zen. The *Ottawa Citizen* publishes a good weekly compendium of events for all age groups and interests; it currently comes out on Saturdays. *Where*, distributed in visitor centres and local hotels, has an excellent calendar of events, as does *Ottawa City Magazine*, produced by the same publisher. Another city magazine, *Ottawa Life*, also runs information about local events.

For free maps and visitor information, stop by the National Capital Commission's **Capital Infocentre** (90 Wellington Street, 239-5000, www.capcan.ca), where you can find out about things to see and do on both sides of the Ottawa River.

Public transportation in the city is relatively efficient and inexpensive. Ottawa's equivalent of a subway is the Transitway, a system of bus-only roads that shuttles people from one end of the city to the other through the downtown core fairly quickly, even in rush hour. From the Transitway, passengers can transfer to local buses running along regular city streets. For information on fares and routes on the

Ontario side of the river, contact OC **Transpo** (741-4390, www.
octranspo.com). On the Quebec side, talk to the Société de transport
de l'Outaouais, or STO (819-770-3242, www.sto.ca).

Finally, a word of caution about some of the city names throughout
this book. In January 2001, Ottawa is due to become a "megacity" in
a merger with a number of other local municipalities, such as Kanata,
Nepean, Gloucester, Vanier, and Rockcliffe Park. However, since locals
will probably still refer to these areas by their soon-to-be old names
for some time to come, despite the edicts of various politicians, I've
retained them here. They might make it a bit easier for you to navigate your way around this sometimes confusing metropolis.

SECRET
ACTIVISTS

The **Ottawa Peace and Environment Resource Centre** (230-4590, www.perc.flora.org) is the organization to call to find out about the latest antinuclear protests and places to wear flowers in your hair. For books on feminism, nonviolent action, environmentalism, macrobiotic cooking, and such, drop in to the **New Octopus Bookstore** (116 Third Avenue, 233-2589).

On the Quebec side of the river, **Terra Flora** (116 Montée St-André, St-André-Avellin, Quebec, 819-985-0894) is an alternative community that often gives guided tours on which people can learn how to live a different kind of life. There's a house made of straw, a solar greenhouse, a greywater recycling system, an organic garden, and all sorts of other projects to check out. The people at Terra Flora really do everything themselves: the children are schooled at home, the community is completely unconnected to the electrical grid, and the toilets are composting models.

SECRET
AFRICAN

Giraffe African Arts (19 Clarence Street, 562-0284) sells handmade gift items from all over Africa, including masks, pottery, musical instruments, fabrics, wall hangings, and all sorts of other loot. It's a great place to go when you want to get something really unusual for a birthday or anniversary gift and don't have a clue what to buy.

S E C R E T
AIRPORT LEAVINGS

The **Unclaimed Luggage and Goods Boutique** (1 Nicholas Street, 241-1190) really does buy most of its inventory of clothes, electronics, books, baby equipment, and luggage from airports and airlines (the rest comes from liquidators and other sources). I think that the people who lose things such as beaded lime-green chiffon evening dresses do so on purpose. But the best deals are on items other than clothes, such as Swiss Army Knives and cell phones. The stock comes from airports all over the world, which would explain the display of Russian nesting dolls and the large quantities of Indian ankle bells. The most fascinating thing about browsing the place is wondering how the stuff came to be here. How did a couple manage to lose both of their wedding bands? What happened to the soldier who misplaced his uniform? Come browse and ponder the vagaries of fate, travel, and baggage handling.

S E C R E T
AL FRESCO

Ottawa's summers are short but sweet, and people here make the most of them. Even before the last bits of muddy snow have melted, you're likely to see university students sunning themselves on the banks of the Rideau Canal in shorts and tank tops (they'll be shivering but determined). And much sooner than sane restaurateurs would dare in more temperate cities, the capital's cafés set up shop outdoors. For most, that means a few rickety tables spread out on the sidewalk. And, while these ersatz patios can be great for people watching, they're usually noisy, uncomfortable, and decidedly unromantic. But there are a few hidden gems that offer a perfect combination: fresh air, a relaxed ambience, and good food. Just be warned that everyone else will find the combination just as appealing, so book ahead and specify that you want an outdoor table.

Bistro 115 (110 Murray Street, 562-7244) is a romantic destination at any time of year. The restaurateurs have created a little slice of France in the Byward Market, with a changing menu of updated continental classics. But in the summer, the terrace in the backyard is a little slice of heaven. About 10 tree-shaded tables, surrounded by containers of black-eyed yellow daisies and a cheerful blue-and-white privacy fence, comprise a candlelit world of their own. You'll hardly know that you're in the heart of the loud, busy market. Expect to linger.

You don't have to go elegant and upscale to get a nice patio, though. The boisterous, down-to-earth Snug Pub, part of the **Heart and Crown** (67 Clarence Street, 562-0674), has a good courtyard for lifting a pint or two. To find it, go down the too cutely named Snug Lane beside the Heart and Crown, overhung with wrought-iron plant hangers and trellises. A huge Guinness sign dominates the patio, which is usually lively late into most nice summer evenings.

I also like the vine-covered deck tucked behind **La Piazza Bistro Italiano** (25 York Street, 562-6666). The pasta, seafood, and steaks here are unremarkable, but the walled patio feels so secluded and special that it makes up for the rather ordinary food.

The take-out food may be so-so, but you can't beat the courtyard of the **West Block** on Parliament Hill, which the great unwashed can enjoy during the summer. Ask the good folks at the National Capital Commission's nearby Info-Tent for directions.

SECRET

ALL NIGHT

So it's 3:30 a.m., and you can't sleep. A few years ago, your options for late-night amusement in Ottawa would have been few. People used to say that the place rolled up its sidewalks at 6 p.m.; the truly unkind said that it never unrolled the sidewalks in the first place. But as the capital has joined the dreaded 24/7 culture, there are suddenly scores of all-night amusements to choose from.

For late-night munchie attacks, downtown all-night restaurants include **Chase Diner** (339 Dalhousie Street, 562-6000), **Bagel Bagel** (92 Clarence Street, 241-8998, all night on Fridays and Saturdays only), **Dunn's Deli** (220 Elgin Street, 230-6444), and **Elgin Street Diner** (374 Elgin Street, 237-9700). Outside the downtown core, 24-hour service is pretty much limited to chain establishments such as **Perkins Family Restaurant** (1130 St. Laurent Boulevard, 747-9190; 1000 Maloney Boulevard, Gatineau, Quebec, 819-561-1000), **Denny's** (2208 Bank Street, 731-4828; 1380 Clyde Avenue, 226-9277; 140 Earl Grey Drive, Kanata, 599-6220), and **Chenoy's** (120 de l'Hôpital, Gatineau, Quebec, 819-561-3354).

After chowing down, you may need a few miles on the treadmill. Try **Florida Fitness** (800 Industrial Avenue, 727-5300, www.florida fitness.ca) or **Gym-Max** (105 Bellehumeur, Gatineau, Quebec, 819-246-0496), both of which are open around the clock. If you're just dropping in to Gym-Max once (as opposed to buying a one-week, two-week, or longer membership), bring your own towel.

Club kids who just don't want the party to end hang out at **Atomic** (137 Besserer Street, 786-1553). Of course, there's no sign. How cool would a place be if *anyone* could find it? Just look for the blank green wall adorned with nothing fancier than a big 137 and a massive steel door. And don't expect much activity before midnight; the place doesn't even open until at least 9 p.m. After paying your cover charge (a couple of bucks on Wednesdays and Thursdays, steeper on the weekends), you'll go down a seemingly endless flight of metal stairs into a long, dim room that gives the eerie impression of a mellow, subterranean railway car. There's also a dance floor upstairs. Some nights, the DJ music pounds and the disco ball glitters until 8 a.m. Other nights, things shut down at the shockingly middle-class hour of 3 a.m. Open Wednesday to Saturday (well, early Sunday morning). Call first, as hours and even the entrance to the building can vary (some nights you'll be asked to use the door at 174 Rideau Street). The info line is also a good source for details on other alternative music events around town.

Gamblers have lots of late-night options. The roulette wheels, slot machines, and craps tables keep humming until 3 a.m., seven nights a week, at the **Casino de Hull** (1 Casino Boulevard, Hull, Quebec, 819-772-2100). But on some Friday and Saturday nights at the **Rideau Carleton Raceway** (4837 Albion Road, Gloucester, 822-2211), you can bet on the ponies until 6 a.m. the next morning. The only trick is that the ponies are televised and are racing half a world away, in Hong Kong. Many of the patrons at Hong Kong night are Asian ex-pats, but the racing forms and commentary are available in both Chinese and English. And, because Hong Kong races tend to feature more horses than their Canadian counterparts, the odds are longer, but the potential payoff is bigger. That draws more than a few starry-eyed non-Asians to the track in the wee hours. There's even free coffee to help you keep your eyes open until the last horse crosses the finish line. Rideau Carleton's general manager got the idea from a racetrack in Vancouver, which had started similar nights to draw in members of that city's large Asian Canadian community. Just call ahead before heading out there to make sure that the races are on that night (the Hong Kong tracks shut down during typhoon season in June, for example). If the Asian ponies aren't running, you can try your luck at the track's slot machines until 3 a.m.

And, finally, if buying a belt sander or comparison shopping for air conditioners is more your idea of late-night kicks, check out the all-night **Home Depot** (1616 Cyrville Road, 744-1700).

SECRET
ANGELS

Annabelle's the Angel Store (1200F Wellington Street, 729-4558), as you can guess from the name, specializes in cherubim and seraphim, in the form of figurines, stained glass, greeting cards, jewellery, calendars, Christmas decorations, and more. There are also stuffed animals, crystals, prisms, CDs, and products related to fairies. Owner Cindy Musat says, "A lot of people come here when they're lost or confused. . . . Half the time I think I'm half therapist." When asked why she opened the store, she says, hesitantly, "I don't know how open-minded you are . . ." and then explains that she first saw an angel in 1995 and has communicated with them ever since. "It's not just a commercial store," she concludes.

I like the mysterious metal angel poking its trumpet out of the shrubbery at the corner of St. Patrick Street and Sussex Drive. No one seems to know who made it or even much about where it came from, although the consensus seems to be that it was once in a cemetery. The Roman Catholic Church gave it to the National Capital Commission in the late 1970s, and it ended up here, watching over crazed drivers trying to navigate through one of the city's more confusing intersections.

SECRET
ANTIQUES

If you're looking for the apropos lamp to light up your vintage life, check out **Yardley's Antiques** (1240 Bank Street, 739-9580). The store also sells pine furniture and pop culture memorabilia, but the glory of the place is its light fixtures, 90% of them reconditioned antiques (every lamp in the shop has been rewired to meet CSA safety standards). There are streamlined 1920s floor lamps, curving Art Nouveau desk lamps, enormous Victorian chandeliers, Tiffany-style lamps with stained-glass shades — pick your decade, and you'll probably find something. And, if lamps aren't your thing, you can always illuminate your rec room with one of the neon beer signs. Bud Light, anyone?

There must be a lot of interest in antique lighting, since Ottawa also supports a second shop specializing in similar old fixtures: the **Architectural Antique Warehouse/Vintage Lighting** (342 Richmond Road, 722-1510).

SECRET
ARCHITECTURE

There's a whole group of federal government buildings that look like remnants from a giant antique castles store. Built of massive blocks of stone, anchored by solid towers, and capped by crenellated battlements that look like the perfect place to let loose a quiver full of arrows, they sometimes puzzle visitors to the city. Was Ottawa ever in danger of invasion by the cast of *Monty Python and the Holy Grail*? No, but in the early 1900s the young capital was desperate to look as worthy and historic as the important cities back in the old country. So the federal department of public works sent chief architect David Ewart to Britain on a grand tour of various castles and country homes. When he came back, he adapted what he'd seen into a unique Ottawa vernacular. Ewart's buildings include the Victoria Memorial Museum, now the **Canadian Museum of Nature** (240 McLeod Street, 566-4700); the **Royal Canadian Mint** (320 Sussex Drive, 993-3500); the **Canadian War Museum** (330 Sussex Drive, 819-776-8600); the **Connaught Building** (Mackenzie Avenue), home of the Canada Customs and Revenue Agency; and the **Dominion Observatory** (Central Experimental Farm). Ewart's own house (464 Besserer Street) is surprisingly simple and subdued.

SECRET
ARMOUR

Ever wanted your own suit of armour? Call the **South Tower Armouring Guild** in Metcalfe, just south of Ottawa (821-1846, www.southtower.on.ca). Bill Fedun has been supplying members of the Society for Creative Anachronism and other history buffs for years. He'll make a chain-mail suit to your specifications or a full suit of armour based on existing suits in major museums. You can also pick up broadswords and other accessories for the well-dressed knight.

S E C R E T
A R T

Since 1990, the annual **Pontiac Artists' Studio Tour** (819-647-3416, mha-net.org/users/pasta) has brought thousands of curious art lovers to the country studios of some 50 artists. Pontiac is a largely rural area of western Quebec that hugs the Ottawa River about an hour west of the capital. And, while the tour is fun, you don't have to wait until June to visit these artists. Call the tour association office at the number above, or check out its web site, for current contact numbers of the painters, sculptors, woodworkers, potters, writers, and other creative souls whose works have been featured on past tours. Then call ahead to make appointments to see their latest works. As well as the opportunity to experience some one-of-a-kind artworks, you'll get to enjoy spectacular views of the river and the Eardley Escarpment as you explore the area.

SECRET
ART DECO

Widdicomb's of Westboro (303 Richmond Road, 722-8321) specializes in mahogany furniture of the 1920s and 1930s. It's a lovely place to browse and pretend that you're an extra in *Brideshead Revisited*. While the bedroom sets, leather-topped desks, dining room tables, and wing chairs won't fit well in a traveller's suitcase or car, you can often pick up smaller decorative accessories from the same era. Two 1936 advertising posters for transatlantic voyages that I spotted a while ago were perfect streamlined examples of the last gasp of Art Deco; they even had unblemished vintage frames.

SECRET
ASTROLABE

One of the coolest artifacts in the **Canadian Museum of Civilization** (100 Laurier Street, Hull, Quebec, 819-776-7000) is a 17th-century navigational instrument called an astrolabe that once belonged to explorer Samuel de Champlain. Lost for centuries, it finally turned up in a farmer's field in the Ottawa Valley, dug up by a plow. It now holds pride of place at the museum. Unfortunately, it didn't fare so well in the hands of sculptor Hamilton MacCarthy, who created the 1915 statue of Champlain that looks out over the city from Nepean Point, behind the National Gallery of Canada. MacCarthy depicted Champlain gazing wisely through the circular instrument, which the famous explorer holds upside down.

SECRET
BAGELS

No less an authority than the *Robb Report*, the magazine of the filthy rich, has called the **Ottawa Bagelshop and Deli** (1321 Wellington Street, 722-8753, www.bagelshop.on.ca) "the best bagel shop in the world." And who am I to disagree? The hand-rolled bagels, baked in a wood-burning oven at the back of the store, are just as dense and chewy as any bagel buff could desire. Founded in 1984, the store now claims to be Canada's largest bagel shop. But there's much more here than just bagels. I love browsing the shelves of gourmet food just for relaxation, daydreaming about what I might cook with products such as cabernet vinegar or apricot honey and tarragon sauce. There's also an excellent deli. You can get sandwiches, salads, and other light meals at the licensed restaurant in the back, where the white chocolate and macadamia nut cookies are to die for.

Much as I love the Ottawa Bagelshop product, I think that it's in a dead heat for the title of world's best bagel with upstart **Kettleman's Bagels** (912 Bank Street and two other locations, 567-7100, www.kettlemansbagel.com). The round-the-clock outlet on Bank Street is a hopping place after consumer shows or hockey games at nearby Lansdowne Park. You get a front-row view of sweaty bagel makers kneading and rolling their product and tossing it into the wood-burning oven that takes up most of the store's space. The bagels are magnificent, and you can get genuine deli accompaniments such as knishes and kosher pickles.

SECRET
BAKERIES

Trillium Bakery (209 Belmont Street, 730-1316 and 1311 Wellington Street, 728-6822) whips up a bewildering variety of loaves, including some suitable for customers with various medical conditions such as diabetes and food allergies. I love the whole-wheat cornmeal bread, a solid loaf that makes the most wonderful toast without being as solid as a brick, as are some "wholesome" loaves.

In the west end, **Great Harvest Bread Company** (194 Robertson Road, Nepean, 820-4052) also cooks up loaves for people allergic to various ingredients, as well as the usual assortment of regular breads, cookies, and pastries.

Wild Oat (817 Bank Street, 232-6232) is a tofu and granola sort of bakery where you can pick up breads baked from organic grains as well as organic pastas, sauces, and vegetables.

SECRET
BASEBALL

I'm not much of a baseball fan, but going to see the **Ottawa Lynx** (JetForm Park, 300 Coventry Road, 749-9947, www.ottawalynx.com) on a warm summer night makes me understand the allure of the game. This Triple A venue is small enough that you can actually see what's going on. It's the kind of place where the parking is more expensive than the tickets; a night out for a family of four could come in under $30, including hot dogs and beer. In fact, it's very family oriented, with lots of entertainment and contests for kids between each inning.

To catch a free game, bike by the diamonds in **Riverain Park** (River Road at McArthur Avenue, Vanier), where some league or other always seems to be playing under the floodlights. If you get bored with the game, wander over to the Rideau River and watch the ducks.

S E C R E T
BEACHES

Deep in the heart of exclusive Rockcliffe Park, there's a — gasp! — public beach at tiny **McKay Lake** (also called **Hemlock Lake** on some maps). Look for the path off Hillsdale Road, between Lansdowne Road North and Sandridge Road. There's a small parking lot on Hillsdale, opposite the lake.

Several people pleaded with me not to tell everyone about **Westboro Beach** (Ottawa River Parkway between Island Park Drive and Woodroffe Avenue), but I am a heartless old thing. A mere 10-minute drive from Parliament Hill, it's a great place to tan and build sand castles. The water may not always be the best for swimming, especially if there's been a lot of rain; call 244-5300, extension 4014, during office hours or 244-5444 after hours for information on water conditions.

For a beach so secret that the National Capital Commission doesn't want you to know about it, head to **Meech Lake** in Gatineau Park. There, near the ruins of the Carbide Willson mill, is an isolated strip of rocky beach that has been home to the capital area's nude sunbathers for more than 60 years. As this book went to press, the naturalists were still in a standoff with the powers that be. Nudists claimed traditional rights to the spot, while government officials waved rule books and protested that unwary families of hikers were stumbling upon the place and getting more nature than they bargained for. So, if you want to soak up some rays in the altogether, check it out — but bring a cover-up just in case. To get there, follow the signs for O'Brien Beach (though O'Brien Beach is not the "clothing optional" spot) and park in lot 11. You'll follow trail 36 for part of your trip. For detailed directions, pick up a copy of the trail map at the park office (33 Scott Road, Chelsea, Quebec, 819-827-2020) and follow the route to the ruins. The nudist beach is not marked.

S E C R E T
BEADS

The **Sassy Bead Company** (757 Bank Street, 567-7886, and 11 William Street, 562-2812) is a fun place to browse for beads as well as finished necklaces, earrings, and beaded clothes. There's also a wide variety of classes in beading.

Canada Beading Supply (200 Colonnade Road South, Unit 4, Nepean, 727-3886, www.canbead.com) is a beading behemoth. Canada's largest wholesaler and retailer of gemstone beads, it sells beads by mail order and at shows across North America. At its showroom headquarters in suburban Nepean, you can check out its entire stock of 5,000 products, which includes more than 100 types of gems as well as freshwater pearls, metal fittings, equipment for beading enthusiasts, and books. The selection of intriguing tiny artworks, such as accent beads made in cloisonné, pewter, silver, or bone, is fun to explore even if you are no more likely to bead a sweater than fly to Mars.

Rainbow Minerals (2615 Lancaster Road, Unit 24, 733-8440, www.rainbowminerals.com) imports and wholesales beads as well as gemstones, fossils, finished jewellery, and all sorts of other cool stuff from Brazil, China, Southeast Asia, South Africa, and the United States. The drag is that it's solely a wholesaler, so you have to be in the gems, minerals, or jewellery business to get a peek.

SECRET

BED AND
BREAKFAST

Natural Choice 4/Nature Vegetarian Bed & Breakfast (263 McLeod Street, 563-4399, www.vegybnb.com) also accommodates weddings, funerals, and massages (hopefully not in that order). It's a homey place where you can take a free yoga class, munch on fresh spelt bread, have a holistic health treatment, or browse through a rack of art cards by local photographers. Bring the whole family: the B&B welcomes kids, cats, and dogs.

The **Cushing Nature Retreat** in rural Quebec (197 Fierobin, Ladysmith, Quebec, 819-647-3226, www.cushing-nature.com) is part B&B, part nature facility; the most intriguing attraction is the birds-of-prey centre, which breeds raptors and cares for injured birds. The retreat's main building, with five guestrooms, and the separate dining hall are on the shores of Indian Lake. Actually, B&B is a bit of a misnomer; packages include both breakfast and a three-course dinner.

SECRET
BIRDING

The bible for local birders is a book called *Nature and Natural Areas in Canada's Capital* by Daniel Brunton, copublished by the *Ottawa Citizen* and the **Ottawa Field-Naturalists Club** (Box 35069, Westgate Post Office, Ottawa, ON, K1Z 1A2, www.achilles.net/ofnc). You can order a copy for five dollars plus postage by writing to the above address. The club also has a birding hotline (860-9000) that provides information on recent sightings.

One of the many great things about Ottawa is how easy it is to get to some excellent wild areas, some of them close to downtown. More than 250 species of waterfowl and woodland birds have appeared in and around **Shirleys Bay**, a west-end site on the Ottawa River. Another rich west-end birding site is the **Britannia Conservation Area**, accessible from Cassels Street near Britannia Road. Herons, vireos, flycatchers, warblers, swallows, hawks, purple martins, and many other species have been spotted here. Gulls congregate near the filtration plant on Britannia Point, which is also the only place in southern Ontario that you're likely to see an arctic tern. Other birding sites nearby include **Lakeside Gardens** and **Andrew Haydon Park**.

If you're headed to the **Stony Swamp Conservation Area**, take some seeds with you; the chickadees here are so tame that they may feed from your hand. In the **Pinhey Forest Reserve** behind the Nepean Sportsplex, keep an eye open for ruffled grouse and owls. The orchards at the **Central Experimental Farm** are a big draw for fruit-eating birds, while the **Mer Bleue Conservation Area** on the east side of the capital attracts marsh birds. On the Quebec side, **Brébeuf Park** is a good place to spot waterfowl. And, naturally enough, **Gatineau Park** is a haven for all kinds of birds.

For several years now, at least one family of **peregrine falcons** has made its home in downtown Ottawa, most recently on a ledge at the top of the **Crowne Plaza** hotel (101 Lyon Street). You can often spot them on or near several buildings in the area, including the Standard Life building, Constitution Square, and the Ottawa Marriott hotel. Volunteers from the Ottawa Field-Naturalists Club keep watch on the chicklets (that's really the term) and post regular reports on their web site. According to the club, urban peregrine falcons with human guardian angels stand an 80% chance of survival — much better odds than their cousins in the wild face.

Birder's Corner (2 Beechwood Avenue, Unit 101, Vanier, 741-0945) and **Wild Birds Unlimited** (1500 Bank Street, 521-7333, www.wbu. com) stock all kinds of goodies for bird lovers, including books, bird baths, feeders, houses, and seeds, as well as stained glass and wind chimes with bird motifs.

The patron saint of Ottawa's wild birds is Kathy Nihei of the **Wild Bird Care Centre** (734 Moodie Drive, Nepean, 828-2849, www. wildbird.cyberus.ca), which she started in 1981. Today the centre cares for some 4,000 injured birds each year and handles about 15,000 telephone inquiries. You can take a self-guided tour of the centre (call first to find out when visiting hours are), and you can support its work by buying a membership.

SECRET
BLUES

One of the best places to hear the blues in Ottawa is at the **Ottawa Bluesfest** (annually in July, 233-8798, www.ottawa-bluesfest.ca). I can say this despite the annual complaints from blues devotees that the festival panders to nonbelievers by signing up headliners of dubious blues value, such as Aretha Franklin and Sting. Maybe Sting is about as bluesy as Barry Manilow is, but he does sell tickets, which makes it possible for the festival to afford more true blues acts. For the past few years, the Bluesfest has been held at Lebreton Flats, and here's my word to the wise: take public transportation to the site. Since it's basically a giant field, the parking facilities are empty lots with no paving, markings, or rights of way, and they create chaos in the hours right before and after a major show — particularly if recent rain has churned up some fresh mud.

It's not much of a secret to locals, but **The Rainbow** (76 Murray Street, 241-5123, www.soundzgood.com/rainbow) has been booking lots of local and international blues acts since 1984. The well-proportioned (small enough to see well, big enough to be comfortable) space on the second floor also plays host to jazz bands and other groups. But if you're in the mood for the blues, your best odds of finding them in the capital are here. This is the place that Dan Aykroyd and Jim Belushi picked recently when they were in town and felt like belting out some Blues Brothers stuff.

For the latest info, contact the **Ottawa Blues Society** (www. soundz good.com/obs/index.html). Society president Mark Hall spins blues on Sunday nights from 10 p.m. until midnight on The Bear FM (106.9).

SECRET
BOG

Due to a quirk of nature that gives it a microclimate typical of more northern regions, the bog at the **Mer Bleue Conservation Area** (Dolman Ridge Road, Gloucester, 239-5000) is home to all sorts of plants that you'd usually find closer to the Arctic. You might also spot wildlife rarities such as the spotted turtle. A boardwalk leads through the bog so that visitors don't trample the fragile sphagnum moss. To get there, take the Innes Road exit from Highway 417. Head left (east) on Innes to Anderson Road, and then turn right (south) on Anderson. A few miles along, you'll see the signs for the conservation area to your left; the parking lot is a mile or so from the intersection.

SECRET
BOOKS

Basilisk Dreams Books (857B Bank Street, 230-2474, www.basilisk.on.ca) specializes in science fiction, horror, and fantasy. As a bonus, it offers 10% to 15% off all books on the current best-seller list in *Locus*, an SF magazine.

Just down the street, **Prime Crime Mystery Bookstore** (891 Bank Street, 238-2583) is co-owned by mystery authors Mary Jane Maffini and Linda Wiken. Look out for the collections of mystery short stories by a group of local authors known as the Ladies' Killing Circle; these popular books always have great titles, such as *Menopause Is Murder.*

As well as having what is probably the city's best selection of new mysteries, the store has shelves of gently used sleuthing books, offered for one-third off their original retail prices. If you like to write mysteries as well as read them, ask the clerk for information about **Capital Crime Writers**.

Collected Works (1242 Wellington Street, 722-1265) is a cozy neighbourhood bookstore where the coffee is always hot and the selection is always slightly unexpected. Two of my other favourite independent bookstores are **Books on Beechwood** (35 Beechwood Avenue, Vanier, 742-5030) and **Leishman Books** (Westgate Shopping Centre, 722-8313).

The largest French-language bookstore on the Ottawa side of the capital region is probably **Librairie du Soleil** (321 Dalhousie Street, 241-6999). Several bookstores specialize in foreign language books, including the **Polish Bookstore in Ottawa** (512 Rideau Street, 789-8260) and **Girol Spanish and Portuguese Books** (120 Somerset Street West, 233-9044). Speaking of foreign languages, if you just can't get enough passive voice and obscure acronyms, check out **Renouf Books** (71 1/2 Sparks Street, 238-8985, www.renouf books.com), which specializes in government, legal, and business publications.

The main level of **Second Time Around** (1083 Wellington Street, 729-8220) is cluttered with 99% junk, such as daisy-wheel printers, wheezy electric organs, and battered toys. But if you pick your way down to the basement, you'll hit pay dirt: shelves and shelves of paperbacks, hardcovers, and children's books, all offered for the princely sum of 10 for a dollar. There's usually a lot of good stuff here if you're willing to root around, including scads of relatively recent political nonfiction and mass-market fiction.

Ex Libris (120 Metcalfe Street, 236-0301) is the Ottawa Public Library's used bookstore. There are good deals on sturdy hardcovers that the library is dropping from its collection. Call first to confirm hours of operation.

SECRET
BOOZE

OK, a store this big probably isn't much of a secret. But you can find some offbeat booze in the **Liquor Control Board of Ontario**'s megastore (275 Rideau Street, 789-LCBO). At 17,000 square feet, it was the biggest liquor store in Ontario when it opened in the spring of 2000.

In Quebec, the powers that be have decreed that adults are mature enough to buy wine and beer in local convenience stores (**dépanneurs**). Of course, the wine that you pluck out of a cooler full of quart bottles of beer and bags of week-old milk probably won't be quite as, shall we say, elegant as the vintages described in wine magazines. But then you don't expect four-star cuisine at a 7-11, do you? You can also buy booze in some grocery stores and other outlets in Quebec.

SECRET
BREAKFAST

You probably won't find many tourists eagerly awaiting weekend breakfast at **Stoneface Dolly's** (479 Bronson Avenue, 230-2088), which is downtown but off the main visitor trail. That's not to say, however, that you won't face a lineup: the fresh juices and goodies such as eggs natasha (basically, eggs florentine with smoked salmon) make the place popular with locals. It's also open for lunch and dinner and offers a range of vegetarian dishes as well as meaty treats.

S E C R E T

BRITISH

Many visitors to Ottawa say that it reminds them of England. I can't see it myself, except perhaps in the gothic exuberance of Parliament Hill. But there are many people with British backgrounds here, which means a ready market for UK-style shops and pubs.

For a wide selection of the latest British books, as well as North American titles, go to **Nicholas Hoare** (419 Sussex Drive, 562-2665). With its sliding bookcase ladders, fireplace, comfy couch, and resident cat, it's a lovely place to browse even if your knowledge of British letters extends no further than Dickens. None of the shelves is labelled; staff trust that you have the sense to realize when you're in the travel section rather than the biography section. And, speaking of the staff, they really know their stuff. I wandered in one day and said, "I'm looking for a biography of four 18th-century English sisters that came out a year or two ago, but I can't remember the title or the author." (Yes, I am every sales clerk's living nightmare.) "Oh, that would be *Aristocrats* by Stella Tillyard," the clerk chirped, immediately retrieving a copy from an upper shelf.

After selecting a good book, pop down the block to the **Earl of Sussex** (431 Sussex Drive, 562-5544) to dip into the book while relaxing in a big wing chair in front of the fireplace. You can dig into British dishes such as steak and kidney pie, washing your meal down with a pint of one of the many brews on tap. There are numerous British-style pubs in Ottawa, particularly in and around the Byward Market; in my humble opinion, this is one of the best.

The **Colonel By Fountain** in Confederation Park (Elgin Street at Laurier Avenue West) is a touch of old England: sculpted in 1845, it stood in Trafalgar Square in London for 103 years before the mother country shipped it out here. We were the ones who renamed it after Ottawa's founder.

S E C R E T
BUNKER

Our country's big shots didn't plan to duck their heads under school desks when the big one came. In 1959, the government began digging a massive hole in a farmer's field near Carp, just west of Ottawa. While the feds insisted that it was a signals installation for the army, speculation ran wild. The four-storey underground Central Emergency Government Headquarters opened in 1961 as an emergency shelter in the event of a nuclear war. Designed to resist a five-megaton blast nearby, it was built on a five-foot-deep gravel pad that would allow the whole building to shift during the explosion. Even the boiler and the air conditioner were mounted on top of giant shock absorbers. The media promptly dubbed the structure the **Diefenbunker** (3911 Carp Road, 839-0007, www.diefenbunker.ca) in honour of Prime Minister John Diefenbaker. It stood at the ready for more than 30 years, a

100,000-square-foot outpost complete with hospital, morgue, Bank of Canada vault, and CBC station, but the only PM who ever visited it was Pierre Elliott Trudeau, who dropped by with Minister of Defence Barney Danson in 1976. The shelter was decommissioned in 1994 and started on the road to its new life as a Cold War museum, which opened in 1998. Today guides, many of them ex-employees of the bunker, take visitors on a one-and-a-half-hour tour.

S E C R E T
BURGERS

Tucked behind the massive Terrasses de la Chaudière office complex, you'll find an unpretentious little restaurant that serves some of the biggest and juiciest burgers in the capital area. At lunchtime, **Café le Twist** (88 Montcalm Street, Hull, 777-8886) is likely to be jammed with public servants fleeing the cafeteria-style takeout joints at Terrasses, so come early to get a seat. And, if you find a burger, salad, and fries way too much for lunch, you're in luck: the burger here comes unadorned with side dishes (though you can order them separately).

S E C R E T
BUSES

Despite the complaints that I have occasionally lobbed its way (usually when it's minus 20 on a January night and every bus in town seems to have disappeared), **OC Transpo** runs a great city bus system. Transportation planners from as far away as Australia have come to study the Transitway, a citywide system of bus-only roads. And, while the Transitway is handy, to my mind the best things about OC Transpo are the web site (www.octranspo.com), where you can get maps and schedules for every route, and the telephone system, which can tell you when each bus is due to arrive at your particular stop (dial 560-1000 plus your stop number, which is found on the sign at the stop). For five dollars at local retailers or six dollars on any city bus, you can buy a one-day pass that gives you unlimited rides on any bus in the system. To get to many of the major tourist spots, take the number-7 route. It goes right by Parliament Hill and the Rideau Centre and as far east as the RCMP Musical Ride Centre. It also takes you within a few blocks of the Canadian Museum of Nature, the National Gallery of Canada, and the Byward Market.

For a different sort of tour, check out the privately run **Amphibus** (Lady Dive Tours, Elgin and Sparks Streets, 852-1132), an oddball conveyance that runs on city streets but also converts to a boat that takes tourists along the Ottawa River.

S E C R E T
CABARET

The floor show at the rambling **Ferme Rouge** restaurant on the eastern edge of the Outaouais (1957 Montreal Road West, Masson-Angers, Quebec, 819-986-7013, www.fermerouge.ca) is hard to categorize: a bit Las Vegas, a bit Céline Dion, a little bit country, a little bit rock and roll. The servers are also performers, taking breaks from clearing tables to kick up their heels in a mad can-can or do their best 1970s lounge-lizard impressions. It's tempting to say that there's nothing else like it in the capital area, but that's not true. There's also **Gilbo's** (651 St. Joseph Boulevard, Hull, Quebec, 819-770-1115), which offers a similar evening out on a smaller scale. Both establishments serve huge lashings of food to go with the entertainment.

S E C R E T
CAMPING

Believe it or not, you can pitch a tent just a half-hour walk or short bike ride from Parliament Hill. **Lebreton Campground** (236-1251 or 239-5000) is for tents only and offers showers, toilets, bike storage, and 24-hour security.

S E C R E T
CAMPING EQUIPMENT

There's no shortage of fancy outdoor equipment stores in Ottawa. In fact, comparison shoppers have a heyday in and around Westboro, where they can shuttle among half a dozen major shops to compare prices on tents, sleeping bags, and hiking boots. Stores there include **Trailhead** (1960 Scott Street, 722-4229, www.trailheadcnd.com), **The Expedition Shoppe** (369 Richmond Road, 722-0166; also

43 York Street, 241-8397), the oddly named **Bushtukah** (206 Richmond Road, 792-1170), and the massive new **Mountain Equipment Co-op** (366 Richmond Road, 729-2700, www.mec.ca). But for sheer atmosphere and history, go to **Irving Rivers** (24 Byward Market Street, 241-1415). It's not hard to spot the building — just look for the huge "We Corner the Market!" sign painted on the wall facing York Street. The store has been here since 1950, and I doubt that the decor or the approach has changed much since then. Every square inch of floor, wall, and ceiling, save the minimum needed to allow customers to circulate, is lined with hats, boots, and camping gear. You can get a lot of the latest high-tech gizmos; however, if you're tired of buying jackets and shoes that come with bigger instruction manuals than today's cars do, you can buy timeless, simple products here too. The staff know their stuff. And, even if you don't buy a thing, you'll have a great time browsing.

SECRET
CANDLES

Doozy Candles (744 Bronson Avenue, 567-6997, www.doozy candle.com), as the name suggests, are pretty amazing. Handmade in a glass-fronted studio on the premises by reconstituted hippie Bruce Langer and business partner Greg Brayford, the candles feature recyclable shells in dazzling colours. The white wax burning inside makes them resemble stained-glass windows. They don't leak or drip, and some burn up to 100 hours. But the store is more than candles: it's a retail statement. Two of Langer's enthusiasms are encouraging hemp cultivation and supporting local producers, so you'll also find Ottawa-made soap, jewellery, greeting cards, artworks, and hemp clothing (that part of the store goes by the name An Acre of Hemp). Meanwhile, Brayford is a musician, so the stone stage that dominates the back of the store plays host to local performers who entertain shoppers on weekend afternoons.

S E C R E T
CARIBBEAN

Groovy's Roti Hut (574 Rideau Street, 789-7939) is a laid-back place where the reggae music is mellow, the Red Stripe beer and guava nectar are cold, and the rotis are hot, juicy, and cheap. You can get chicken, conch, goat, and other kinds of rotis or other Jamaican fare such as curried snapper or rice and peas. Take your choice home, sit down for a quick bite in the small front room with its bright, multi-coloured walls, or settle down in the larger restaurant at the back.

S E C R E T
CATS

At least among locals, Ottawa's worst-kept secret is René Chartrand, the genial gentleman who has become known as the **Cat Man of Parliament Hill**. In a small compound tucked behind the wrought-iron fence west of the Centre Block, Chartrand feeds a ragtag collection of feral cats that have lived in the wooded area behind the hill since the late 1970s. Since 1987, he has trekked to the hill twice a day to dole out kibble, having taken over from the original Cat Lady, the late Irene Desormeaux. In the past few years, the enterprise has expanded from its casual roots: the cats now hang out in wooden shelters in the shape of the Parliament buildings, and a permanent bilingual sign explains that the whole shebang costs some $6,000 a year (there are discreet donation boxes affixed to the railings). It's a completely private, grassroots thing and seems to drive the official guides nuts; they usually skip the enclosure altogether unless an unruly tourist wanders over and asks about it.

SECRET
CAVES

West Quebec is the place for spelunkers in the nation's capital. Experts estimate that the **Laflèche Caves** (Highway 307 between Wakefield and Val des Monts, 819-457-4033) are over 12,000 years old. To see the rock formations, bat colonies, and unusual plants here, you need to reserve a space on one of the tours. Meanwhile, in Gatineau Park, you can guide yourself through the **Lusk Caves** near Lac Philippe. However, if you're going to visit these caverns of eroded marble, the park office strongly advises you to wear well-treaded shoes and protective headgear and to bring a flashlight. For a map and detailed directions, contact the park visitor centre (33 Scott Road, Chelsea, Quebec, 819-827-2020).

SECRET
CEMETERIES

Founded in 1873, the rambling **Beechwood Cemetery** (280 Beechwood Avenue, 741-9530) is both a peaceful haven and a crash course in Ottawa's (and Canada's) history. Consider the plaque for political social crusader Tommy Douglas, with its stirring epitaph: "Courage my friends, 'tis not too late to make a better world." Prime Minister Robert Borden is buried here, with a rough stone cross and marker that are somewhat overshadowed by the large historical plaque nearby. Sir Sandford Fleming, inventor of standard time and longtime Ottawan, lies beneath a large, twisted Manchurian lilac, surrounded by his extended family. Despite the detailed brochure provided at the office, it's not an easy place to navigate; I've looked in vain for poet Archibald Lampman's grave. The cemetery, founded as a Protestant counterpoint to the nearby Notre Dame cemetery, now reflects just about every ethnic group that has passed through the city.

One of the oldest cemeteries in the city is found on the grounds of the **Billings Estate Museum** (2100 Cabot Street, 247-4830). Part of the cemetery was for the exclusive use of the Billings family, the wealthy local dynasty on whose property the cemetery was; the rest was available to the entire community of Billings Bridge. The oldest grave dates back to 1820, while the last member of the founding family laid to rest there was buried in 1961. Records show that 140 people are buried at the site, but numerous tombstones have been damaged or destroyed. The museum recently repaired many of the stones of the Billings family, and these are now on display in a building on the grounds. Most of the stones are engraved with a weeping willow, the symbol of both sorrow and everlasting life.

SECRET
CERAMICS

For vases, pitchers, and plates that are more decorative than useful, tread carefully into the artsy **Gallery Lynda Greenberg** (13 Murray Street, 241-2767). To express your creativity on ready-to-paint wares — or to let out the latent artistic genius in your child — go to **The Mud Oven** (1065 Bank Street, 730-0814) or **Gotta Paint** (382 Richmond Road, 729-7754).

SECRET
CEREMONIAL ROUTES

Throughout the city's history, civic-minded Ottawans have decried the capital's lack of a mall that would link our national institutions to each other. At the turn of the century, there were grand plans to build a ceremonial route from the governor general's residence at Rideau Hall to Parliament Hill. The elegant **Minto Bridges** (behind Ottawa City Hall) across the Rideau River were built before plans to upgrade King Edward Avenue fell apart. Today the bridges have been restored, but King Edward is still a traffic-clogged artery that has seen better days.

The latest attempt to give Ottawa a grand boulevard has been the National Capital Commission's "**Confederation Boulevard**" — a good idea on paper that is rather confusing in reality. The problem is that Confederation Boulevard doesn't appear on any map save those published by the commission. It's actually a circular route covering both sides of the river along several existing streets and two bridges, but I can't tell you how many times frustrated tourists have pulled over to ask me where Confederation Boulevard is, waving their non-commission maps in frustration.

SECRET
CHEAP HOTELS

Don't expect 24-hour room service, a chocolate on your pillow, or even peace and quiet in some cases. But for cheap sleeps fairly close to downtown, try the **Concorde Motel** (333 Montreal Road, Vanier, 745-2112) or the **Richmond Plaza Motel** (238 Richmond Road, 722-6591). You can also get a bed for the night for about $20 at the **Ottawa International Hostel** (75 Nicholas Street, 235-2595, www.hostellingintl.on.ca).

SECRET
CHEFS

Le Cordon Bleu Culinary Arts Institute — the only one in Canada and the first one established outside France — just moved into a heritage mansion in Sandy Hill (453 Laurier Avenue East, 236-2433, www.lcbottawa.com). The site is more fitting for Le Cordon Bleu's image than the cramped quarters in a suburban strip mall that the school occupied until recently. As well as courses for professional chefs, Le Cordon Bleu offers weekend classes in esoteric specialties such as pastry making. And, if you don't want to cook at all, you can enjoy the fruits of someone else's labours in the school's new public restaurant.

Downtown at **Domus Café** (85 Murray Street, 241-6007), chef-owner John Taylor makes magic with his take on "Canadian regional cuisine." Just about everything on the menu, which changes daily, is likely to be inventive, intriguing, and good (though not necessarily cheap). If the mere mention of grilled Ontario bobwhite quail with red onion jam, or risotto with scallions and black truffle, is enough to make you salivate, this might be your place. Be warned, though, that the wrought-iron chairs in the spare and elegant dining room can get a bit uncomfortable after a long nosh.

If you like the way things are done at Domus, check out **Juniper** (1293 Wellington Street, 728-0220). Run by two Domus alumni, this west-end restaurant also features an ever-changing menu of eclectic dishes. If anything, the combinations of ingredients are even more exotic here than at Domus, and those with less adventurous palates might find it all a bit too much. But the restaurant has been garnering raves from critics ever since it opened; even the notoriously snooty American magazine *Wine Spectator* deigned to give Juniper's cellar an award.

SECRET
CHILDHOOD

In the children's play area at the **Currency Museum** (245 Sparks Street, 782-8914), children can pretend to be monarchs on coins by dressing up in Julius Caesar-style togas or imitation British royal family robes. Kids also love the locomotives and hands-on exhibits at the **National Museum of Science and Technology** (1867 St. Laurent Boulevard, 991-3044), and the vintage planes at the **National Aviation Museum** (Aviation and Rockcliffe Parkways, 993-2010).

SECRET
CHILDREN'S CLOTHES

Local clothier **Kid's Cosy Cottons** (517 Sussex Drive, 562-2679 or 300 Earl Grey Drive, Kanata, 599-6299, www.kidscosycottons.com) has a devoted following of families who love the company's tough but trendy mix-and-match pants, shorts, tops, and skirts for kids under 12. But here's the secret: hit the company's warehouse (2620 Lancaster Road, Units A and B, 523-2679), near the National Museum of Science and Technology, for deals on last year's lines and overstocks. Call ahead to find out when end-of-season sales are.

SECRET
CHINESE

Thursday nights at the **Shanghai Restaurant** (351 Somerset Street West, 233-4001) have been shaking up Chinatown lately. Starting about 9 p.m., DJs Linus and Todd spin everything from funk and hip hop to lounge music — anything that creates a laid-back atmosphere for the 20-somethings who flock here to enjoy dim sum by candlelight and disco ball. Co-owner Don Kwan borrowed the "Shanghai beats" concept from San Francisco, where it has taken off in a number of Chinese restaurants. The warm red walls, rotating art exhibits, and trendy drinks such as the Shangtini combine to make this one cool nightspot. With just 50 seats or so, though, the place often fills up fast. Come early, lean back, and get into the groove.

Just down the street from Shanghai, **Yang Sheng** (662 Somerset Street West, 235-5794) doesn't look like much, but it has a citywide reputation for its barbecued duck. Outside Chinatown, the family-run **Mitzi's Dining Lounge** (1300 Bank Street, 523-1065) attracts a devoted following in Ottawa South with its hot-and-sour soup. It's another place where the food counts for more than the decor. Meanwhile, the **Palais Imperial** (311-313 Dalhousie Street, 789-6888) in the Byward Market is popular for its all-day dim sum.

In 1999, two intriguing Chinese furniture stores opened just blocks from each other in Ottawa South. **The Middle Kingdom** (1099 Bank Street, 730-3621, www.middlekingdomonline.com) sells a mixture of antique and reproduction pieces as well as textiles, porcelain, bronze, art, and jewellery. Down the block, **The China Connection** (1181 Bank Street, 730-3779) sells large pieces of 19th- and 20th-century Chinese furniture, most from middle-class or upper-middle-class homes rather than aristocratic residences. Materials include northern elm, pine, birch, and walnut. But my favourite items are the small things: the modern silk purses and pillows appliquéd with 1920s embroidery, for example, or the 1950s-vintage Mao alarm clocks. Co-owner Dina Milne is a fount of information about each piece.

S E C R E T
CHIP WAGONS

When you're sick of healthy tofu dishes and snooty waiters, go for the low-stress, high-cal alternative: lunch from a chip wagon. There are dozens of these short-order kitchens on wheels scattered around the capital, most of them serving a similar menu of hot dogs, hamburgers, pogos, and, of course, fries. If you're feeling really adventurous, try poutine, a Québécois specialty of chips topped with cheese curds and covered in hot, salty gravy. It's a cholesterol bomb in a box and not everyone's cup of potatoes. Two of the most popular chip wagons in town are **Lou's** (Laurier Avenue west of Kent Street or Metcalfe Street at Queen Street), with its can't-miss-it artwork of the eponymous Lou and its crispy, delectable fries, and the **Blooming Onion** (Dalhousie Street at York Street), a favourite with famished late-night club hoppers in the Byward Market.

Closely related to chip wagons, sausage carts spring up all over central Ottawa as soon as the last snow melts. You can't walk a block in the downtown core without finding someone barbecuing bratwurst. As always, though, the trendy Glebe does things a little differently: at the hot-dog wagon outside the Scotiabank (Bank Street at Fourth Avenue), you can get curried chicken or vegetarian hot dogs as well as more usual fare.

SECRET
CHOCOLATE

All the desserts look delectable at **Cakes by Tatiana** (1202 Bank Street, 523-2112). But Dina across the street at The China Connection urged me to try the chocolate champagne corks first, and I haven't made it any further into the merchandise. About the size of a big paperback book and shaped like their namesake, they're hunks of chocolate cake dipped in Belgian chocolate and filled with some sort of soft chocolate centre. Tatiana also makes a wicked-looking Black Forest cake about half a foot deep.

Diabetics, of course, usually don't have much selection when it comes to sweets. But at **Karen's Chocolates** (Westgate Shopping Plaza, 729-9918), there is an entire display case of sugar-free chocolates. A sign warns dieters that the treats are no less fattening than their sugared twins; the sugar substitute used has roughly the same calories as the real stuff, and the candies contain all the fats and oils that make traditional chocolate so addictive. And it seems that the sugar-free alternative is addictive too: one regular customer makes a 50-mile drive to Karen's once a month or so and loads up with $40 worth of treats at a time.

SECRET
CIGARS

So it's 5 a.m., and you're craving a fine smoke to start your day. But the humidor's empty! Fear not; **Comerford's Cigar Store** (124 Bank

Street, 232-7448) opens at 4:30 a.m. on weekdays and at 5 a.m. on Saturdays (closed Sundays). Comerford's has been catering to Ottawa nicotine addicts since 1948, and it's one of the only places in the city where you can actually buy a spittoon. You can also pick up cigar snuffers, humidors, and magazines.

Nighthawks, on the other hand, may have to make do with the smaller but adequate choice of cigars at **Byward Market News** (4 Byward Market, 562-2580), open until 11 p.m. most nights and until 1 a.m. some evenings in the summer. Or, if they like to smoke and boogie at the same time, they can indulge both urges at **The Factory** (160 Rideau Street, 241-6869), a downtown dance club that also boasts a humidor as well as a cigar room with leather couches and a fireplace.

If that sounds too noisy and bourgeois, there's a tiny private smoking lounge at the back of the **Cuban Connection** (110B Clarence Street, 789-2447, www.ottawacigars.com). When I asked about it, the clerk lowered her voice to a confidential whisper. It holds only 16 people, she explained, and you have to be a member to get in. On top of that, there's a waiting list for those who want to join the favoured smoky few. However, even if you don't make the cut to enter the back room, it's worth dropping in to peruse the selection of more than 20,000 stogies, as well as lighters, ashtrays, pipes, and humidors.

SECRET
CLIMBING

Can't get to the mountains? For five dollars, you can scale the 45 multicoloured feet of the climbing wall at **Cyberdome** (St. Laurent

Shopping Centre, 1200 St. Laurent Boulevard, 742-6540, www.cyber dome.ca). The scenic view of the parking garage may not compare with the wide-open vistas of the Rockies, but at least the big windows let in a lot of natural light. And, when you get bored with the physical effort, you can indulge in virtual skateboarding, auto racing, baseball, or skiing.

SECRET COFFEE

I don't drink the stuff. I know that it's a shocking admission for a writer (I don't smoke either, but I'm not averse to booze, so I guess that I'm not a complete loss to my trade). Since I'm such a useless judge of a good cup of java, I've had to rely on insider tips from genuine junkies. Here's the scoop.

A friend of mine swears by the brew at **Planet Coffee** (99 Rideau Street, 789-6261), a place that even non-coffee drinkers will like. Despite the Rideau Street address, its enormous window fronts onto George Street, offering a great panorama of the passing Byward Market parade of fashion victims, club kids, and tourists. The clerks have cool tastes in music too.

Trendy **Fahrenheit** (1169 Bank Street, 730-9829) in Ottawa South has its fans, while at **Lava Java** (124 Osgoode Street, 565-9274) you can quaff specialty coffees while doing your laundry. If you prefer to brew your own, check out the latest espresso and cappuccino machines at the **Italian Gift Shop** (795 Gladstone Street, 233-3719).

And, in this age of reduce, reuse, and recycle, it was only a matter of time before someone discovered the potential of coffee grounds. But the only place where I've found the java log — a fireplace log made from someone's latte leavings — is **Art Beats International** (St. Laurent Shopping Mall, 1200 St. Laurent Boulevard, 746-5884, and 263 Richmond Road, 722-3128). By the way, the shop also stocks nifty gifts, such as glassware from Swaziland and stone sculptures from Zimbabwe.

SECRET
COMPUTERS

If the mere thought of opening up your computer and poking around in its innards makes you queasier than watching surgery videos on PBS, then perhaps the **Northern Micro Factory Outlet** (32 Colonnade Road North, 226-1117, www.northernmicro.com) isn't for you. But chipheads with some do-it-yourself savvy can pick up deals on end-of-the-line components from Northern Micro, one of Canada's largest independent PC companies. The outlet also buys surplus stuff from other manufacturers.

SECRET
CROATIAN

Carling Avenue seems to be a Croatian strip, with two rib-sticking Croatian restaurants vying for your patronage, **Dalmacia Restaurant**

(1702 Carling Avenue, 728-0000) and the **New Dubrovnik** (1170 Carling Avenue, 722-1490). The food at both places is very hearty; after having dinner one night at the New Dubrovnik, I was convinced that I would never eat again.

S E C R E T
CROISSANTS

According to a poll conducted in 2000 by the *Ottawa Citizen*, the best croissants in town are the exquisite but pricey confections sold by **The French Baker** (119 Murray Street, 789-7941). I have to agree — they're flaky, sweet, and worth every last cent of the $1.25 price. The runner-up was the croissant offered by **Baelde Pastry** (53 York Street, 241-8418) for one dollar.

S E C R E T
CYBERCULTURE

You don't have to lug around a big laptop just to check your e-mail. Sit down with a cup of coffee and connect to cyberspace at **AE Micro Internet Café** (288 Bank Street, 230-9000, www.aemicrosystems. com), which bills itself as the largest I-café in town with 25 terminals. The accent is heavy on the Internet and light on the café, which doesn't consist of much more than a small counter at the back. The terminals are separated by semicircular partitions that look a bit like huge film reels. They provide privacy, but they also make the cubicles weirdly reminiscent of those phone rooms where lawyers confer with their imprisoned clients on TV cop shows.

SECRET
CYCLING

There are plenty of regular bike-rental shops in town, but you can also rent adult scooters, mopeds, tandem bikes, and chainless bikes at **Cyco's** (5 Hawthorne Street, 567-8180, or 780 Baseline Road, 226-7277). **RentABike** (1 Rideau Street, in the garage behind the Chateau Laurier, 241-4140, www.cyberus.ca/~rentabike) will rent you tandem bikes and children's trailers. The less athletically inclined can check out the electric bikes and miniscooters at **Electric Drive Cycles** (booth on Sparks Street at Bank Street, 728-2226, www.electricdrive. net).

Finding a spot to lock your bike in the Byward Market is harder than finding an open table at one of the sidewalk cafés, especially on summer weekends. In the summer, Ottawa runs a supervised bike parking lot (William Street at Rideau Street, 244-5300, extension 3225). It's only open from 8:30 a.m. to 5:30 p.m., and it will cost you between one and two dollars to leave your bike there.

If you don't fancy paying for bike parking, but you don't want to lock your bike to a parking meter, there are other options. The bike rack in **Jeanne d'Arc Court**, the courtyard between Clarence and York Streets just east of Sussex Drive, is securely bolted to the ground and often empty. One drawback is that the court isn't particularly busy, so it might be tempting for bicycle thieves. And make sure to get your bike before 11 p.m., when the court's gates are locked for the night.

OC Transpo (741-4390, www.octranspo.com) recently installed bike racks on the buses serving some of its busiest downtown routes, including most buses numbered 2, 95, and 97. You can load your bike for free as long as there's room. As the bus approaches, just signal your intentions to the driver (advanced skills in mime come in handy here). The rack is on the front of the bus.

Mountain bikers tear along the trails that snake through the undeveloped area of Kanata Lakes. **Kunstadt Sports** (462 Hazeldean Road, Kanata, 831-2059, www.kunstadt.com) often organizes bike races there on Wednesdays; call for dates, times, and directions. To explore the trails on your own, take the Palladium Drive exit from the Queensway. Instead of turning toward the Corel Centre, head north on Huntmar Drive to Richardson Sideroad. Turn right on Richardson Sideroad, then left onto Goulbourn Forced Road. There is a small parking lot near the intersection that gives you access to some of the trails.

There are more than 100 miles of paved bike paths in the capital area. You can pick up an excellent bike map at the National Capital Commission's **Capital Infocentre** (90 Wellington Street, 239-5000). The regional government also publishes a map showing cycling routes and bike lanes on city streets. It's available in local shops or at the **Regional Municipality of Ottawa-Carleton** (111 Lisgar Street, 560-1335, www.rmoc.on.ca/travelwise).

S E C R E T
DIPLOMATS

The Department of Foreign Affairs and International Trade recently started giving tours of its enormous headquarters, the **Lester B. Pearson Building** (125 Sussex Drive, 992-9541, www.dfait-maeci. gc.ca). Built between 1968 and 1973, the building is named for the late minister of foreign affairs (and later prime minister) who won a Nobel Peace Prize for his efforts to solve the Suez Crisis in the 1950s.

There are more than 100 foreign diplomatic missions scattered around Ottawa. Many countries have two properties: the embassy office and the ambassador's home. You can find the addresses of the former simply by looking in the Ottawa *Yellow Pages* under "Embassies." Both buildings are often quite grand. In fact, embassies have been the salvation of many old Victorian mansions that would otherwise have fallen victim to the wrecker's ball, subdivision, or some other dire fate. The **Hungarian Embassy** (306 Metcalfe Street), for example, was built in 1896 for a local merchant. The **Turkish Embassy** (197 Wurtemburg Street) began as a bureaucrat's mansion in 1869 and was later a children's hospital before Turkey bought it in 1953. And **Stadacona Hall** (395 Laurier Avenue East), built for a lumber baron about 1871, was the residence of the French and Belgian ambassadors, successively, before the high commissioner of Brunei moved in.

You can't miss the new **American Embassy**, which stretches along several blocks on the west side of Sussex Drive in the Byward Market. To spot the others, look for four dead giveaways: a national coat of arms near the doorway, an unfamiliar flag flapping from the pole on the lawn, a car with red-and-white diplomatic plates in the driveway, and red parking signs at the curb reading "Diplomatic Loading Zone" (as though ambassadors arrive in large trucks, like furniture or potatoes).

The neighbourhood with the highest density of ambassadorial residences is probably tony **Rockcliffe Park**; others include **Sandy Hill** and **Island Park**.

SECRET
DOLLS

Miniature enthusiasts — not peppy short people but people who create dollhouses — hang out at **Lilliput** (9 Murray Street, 241-1183). As well as debating the merits of a bewildering variety of tiny Sheraton tables, wineglasses, potted plants, and kitchenware, you can pick up magazines, dollhouse kits, and information on hobby shows.

SECRET
DRIVING

Ottawa is a hellish city to get around in, and don't let any enthusiastic tourism promoter tell you differently. The downtown core straddles two rivers, one canal, and two provinces, so it's physically daunting to traffic planners. And there are so many levels of government running the place, each with its own ideas about who should turn where, park where, and stop where. As a result, the city is choked with poorly marked turnoffs, lanes that disappear without warning, and mysterious concrete islands that extend for miles. Many of the streets in the core are one-way thoroughfares, and many in the Byward Market aren't worth driving on most of the time, no matter what direction they go in, because they're so clogged with people, cars, bicycles, rickshaws, and fruit stands.

There are only two freeways on the Ottawa side of the capital area, and one of them (Highway 416) is simply a route out of town. Not surprisingly, the major cross-town multilane highway, the **Queensway**, is a war zone. Avoid it at rush hour at all costs, or you'll find yourself dialling the "How's my driving?" number of the 18-wheeler in front of you just to have someone to talk to.

But there are alternatives to the Queensway and to bumper-to-bumper major arteries. They may not be any faster in rush hour, but at least they're more scenic. On most of them, trucks are banned. And, outside rush hour, they're great fun to drive. From the west, use the **Ottawa River Parkway** as a substitute for the Queensway or Carling Avenue. In the east, the **Rockcliffe Parkway** is a dandy alternative to the Queensway, while the **Aviation Parkway** beats Blair Road any day. If you're coming into town from the airport, pick up **Colonel By Drive** just north of Carleton University for an awesome approach to the downtown core. You'll drive along the Rideau Canal and then suddenly come around a corner to see the canal flanked on one side by the fairy-tale turrets of the Chateau Laurier and on the other side by the Peace Tower. Note that some of these roads are closed to automobile traffic (but are open to cyclists, pedestrians, and in-line skaters) on Sunday mornings throughout the summer; call 239-5000 for details.

For information on road conditions and major closures, call the **Ontario Ministry of Transportation** (city information, 747-0611; eastern Ontario, 1-800-267-0284; whole province, 1-800-268-1376; general information, 1-800-268-4686).

SECRET
ELVIS

Off Churchill Avenue, just south of Richmond Road, keep your eyes open for a city street sign on **Elvis Lives Lane**. The street, officially designated by city council, is named in honour of the tongue-in-cheek Elvis Sighting Society, which meets irregularly at the nearby **Newport Restaurant** (334 Richmond Road, 722-9322) and engages regularly in all sorts of community good works. Founded as a joke on April Fool's Day 1989 by buddies Ervin Budge, Newport owner Moe Attalah, and sports writer Earl MacRae, the society has become a beloved Ottawa in-joke. Attalah claims not to open the letters to the king that arrive from all over the world; after all, they're addressed to Elvis, not to Attalah. Inside the restaurant, every wall surface is covered with Elvis posters, albums, clocks, and dolls. The casual atmosphere and good, basic menu make the Newport a great place for families. And it seems that Elvis mania is slowly creeping through the neighbourhood: next door, the Douvris Martial Arts Academy claims on its front window that "Elvis trains here."

SECRET
EROTICA

For sheer chutzpah, you have to admire **Boutique Erotica** (22 Eddy Street, Hull, 777-4069). For years, the store doggedly hung on to its prime location across the street from the elegant Canadian Museum of Civilization, to the consternation of prudish culture vultures. Finally, the owners moved the shop to a street directly across from a major government office complex, the Terrasses de la Chaudière. From that spot, it now purveys its selection of peek-a-boo lingerie and xxx videos.

The innocuous sign outside **Samantha's Boutique** (386-C Bank Street, 234-6169, www.samanthaslingerie.com) decorously proclaims "Lingerie and Swimwear." But wander down the stairs into the tiny basement shop, and you'll find sky-high stilettos, leather, vinyl, feathers, and a catalogue of French-maid outfits that would put Frederick's of Hollywood to shame. The owner is friendly and enthusiastic, and the place has more the feel of a raunchy home-shopping party than a den of iniquity.

SECRET
ESPIONAGE

Eat your heart out, John Le Carré. The first hints of the East-West enmity that would define the latter half of the 20th century emerged not in Berlin or Moscow or London but here in humble Ottawa. On September 5, 1945, a 26-year-old cipher clerk at the Russian Embassy named **Igor Gouzenko** left the legation with 109 sheets of paper proving that the Soviets were running spy rings in Canada. He'd decided to defect. Not trusting the police, he took his loot to the *Ottawa Journal*. In a decision that would haunt the paper for decades, the editors branded him a kook and sent him home. So he went to the Department of Justice. In a classic case of Ottawa bureaucracy, a commissionaire there told Gouzenko that the place was closed and that he should come back the next day. After some more fruitless attempts the next day to get someone interested in his papers, a terrified Gouzenko returned to his apartment at 511 Somerset Street West. Finally, he got some police protection, just before the Russians battered down the door of his apartment. Eventually, the papers that he'd stolen at the risk of his life led to the arrest and conviction of a number of Soviet spies. The apartment building itself, an ugly brick building with mean little round windows, still squats next to the beer store on the north side of the street, between Bay and Lyon Streets.

Even James Bond made a fictitious visit to the capital. In the collection of short stories *For Your Eyes Only*, Bond comes to town as part of his efforts to track down an ex-Nazi. He drops in at the RCMP headquarters, then located in the **Justice Building** (239 Wellington Street). Author Ian Fleming describes the building as "a massive block of grey masonry built to look stodgily important and to withstand the long and hard winters," but it's unclear whether he himself ever visited Ottawa. Some speculate that he may have come to the city while in Canada to attend Camp X, a wartime spy-training school in southern Ontario.

SECRET
FANTASY

Local author **Charles de Lint** has written more than 40 books of what he describes as "mythic fiction," his own unique style that combines modern settings with folktales and magic. His book *Moonheart*, published in 1984, is a fantasy cult classic set in Ottawa. Tamson House, the location where much of the book's action takes place, is completely fictitious. But de Lint sited Tamson House in an actual park at the corner of Bank Street and Patterson Avenue. I like to think that the house really is there; we just can't see it.

SECRET
FASHIONS

The clothes at **Farah** (275 Richmond Road, 759-8333, www.Farah Online.com) seem to reflect Ottawa's public personality to a T. There are classically cut jackets, pants, and dresses in natural fabrics such as linen and cotton, but most of them have a few funky touches that say "I'm not just a bureaucrat's suit, you know." You might find a simple linen dress with large, bright, fabric-covered buttons or a conservatively cut jacket whose sleeves are made of patterned chiffon. Many items are done in Persian leather or suede. And, if you don't see what you want, you can get something custom made.

If you have champagne tastes and a beer budget, you can pick through the fashion leavings of the Rockcliffe elite at **Clothes Encounters**

of a Second Time (67 Beechwood Avenue, 741-7887). Unlike many consignment stores, it may carry last year's hot cocktail dress or a snazzy Chanel suit. The prices aren't exactly Wal-Mart's, but they're a bargain compared with the original stickers on some of the items.

SECRET
FIREWALKING

Wayne Cadeau says that firewalking calms and focuses the mind. He first tried it in the mid-1980s in California (where else?) and says that it changed his life. Now he's on a mission to help others grow through firewalking at his **Cadeau Institute** (613-735-6574). He frequently offers events and seminars in Ottawa, or you can take a firewalking class in his backyard in the Ottawa Valley town of Pembroke. The idea behind firewalking is that you focus your mind so that your feet don't get burned when you stroll across hot coals. Cadeau has made more than 1,300 crossings. He says that firewalking reduces stress and helps practitioners to take control of their lives. "It's all about turning fear into personal power," he says. I think that I'd rather stick with the fear, but that's just me.

SECRET
FIRST NATIONS

Victoria Island, a small chunk of land in the Ottawa River in the shadow of Parliament Hill, has been a traditional meeting place for local Algonquins for centuries. In 1995, a group of Aboriginal Canadians protesting new tax rules began occupying the island. The protest lasted more than four years, until the National Capital Commission evicted the last 14 protesters. In a neat twist to the story, a local firm called **Turtle Island Tourism Company** (12 Stirling Avenue, 564-9494, www.aboriginalexperiences.com) now runs an Aboriginal tourism centre on the island in the summer. Visitors can buy crafts, watch dancing and drumming, tour a reconstructed summer village, and chow down on game dishes, bannock, and wild rice. To get there on foot or by bike, take the Portage Bridge, which runs off Wellington Street just west of the National Library of Canada. By car, follow Booth Street to the Chaudière Bridge. Don't miss the large totem pole on the eastern tip of the island, carved by BC Native artist Walter Harris in 1985.

Each spring, the **Odawa Native Friendship Centre** (12 Stirling Avenue, 722-3811, www.odawa.on.ca) holds the **Odawa Pow Wow** at the Ottawa-Nepean Tent and Trailer Park (411 Corkstown Road, Nepean). This large event draws drummers, hoop dancers, storytellers, artisans, and others from across North America for a three-day weekend of events. It's one of the highlights of the friendship centre's cultural program, but the centre is also a clearinghouse for information on other Aboriginal events taking place in Ottawa throughout the year.

Baco Restaurant and Wine Bar (200 Beechwood Avenue, 747-0272) serves Native-inspired dishes that showcase traditional foods such as corn, beans, and squash (the "three sisters" of Aboriginal cooking), as well as nuts, seeds, and wild rice. The menu includes some text in Native languages and retellings of Aboriginal legends related to food. Chef and co-owner Joseph Turenne — a 13th-generation Canadian whose family hit these shores in the 1600s — started researching Native cuisine when he worked at the Chateau Laurier helping to assemble a Canada Day menu. He became fascinated with the idea of promoting Canadian cuisine based on indigenous ingredients. "A lot of times, when people think of Canadian cuisine, they think of maple syrup and poutine," he says with a laugh. He works with local farmers, cheese makers, and other suppliers, who often grow or make particular items at his request. Even the wine list is 100% Canadian.

A **Kwakiutl totem pole** from British Columbia lurks in the trees of Confederation Park (Elgin Street at Laurier Avenue West). Created by Kwakiutl artist Henry Hunt in 1971, it's part of a series of totem poles that the government of British Columbia gave to each province and territory to mark the 100th anniversary of British Columbia joining Confederation. Another Kwakiutl artist, Simon Dick, created the enormous thunderbird sculpture known as *Kolus* in 1986 as part of Canada's pavilion at Expo '86 in Vancouver; it now stands guard on the grounds of the Canadian Museum of Civilization.

At the **Indian Art Centre** (10 Wellington Street, Hull, 819-997-6550, www.inac.gc.ca), run by the federal department of Indian and Northern Affairs Canada, you can buy pieces by Native artists, research a particular artist's work in the extensive library, or simply view the latest exhibition, which changes each month. It's open Monday to Friday during office hours.

S E C R E T
FISHING

What I know about fishing would fit on the head of a pin. So don't ask me; ask the experts. A pro fisherman runs the shop at **Britannia**

Bait (2981 Carling Avenue, 829-5387). And **Brightwater Flyfishing** (336 Cumberland Street, 241-6798, www.brightwaterflyfishing.com), which sells equipment and offers courses for fisherpeople from novice to master, is owned by the captain of Canada's flyfishing team.

S E C R E T

FLEA MARKETS

The **Stittsville Flea Market** (Hazeldean Road, Stittsville, 836-5612) is an enormous glorified garage sale — "the largest indoor/outdoor flea market in Eastern Ontario," according to its promotions — that draws hundreds of vendors and hordes of shoppers every Sunday. It's part street theatre, part county fair, and part bargain basement: even if you don't buy anything, it's a hoot to browse through the staggering range of goods available. There are macramé plant hangers that will take you back to 1975, model planes made from pop cans, wooden back scratchers, and antiques of all sorts. One stall sells nothing but exquisitely embroidered rayon sundresses from India, while another specializes in unfinished wooden deacon's benches. Even if you come looking for nothing in particular, you'll probably walk away with a bit of everything in general.

Deep in the heart of an industrial park, the **Bentley Flea Market** (145 Bentley Avenue, Nepean, 225-5613) is open Sundays only. It's a great place to buy stuff for the cottage, from used paperbacks for half a buck and coffee mugs for a buck to bits of old furniture. There's also the usual range of flea market finds, such as Lipton Tea figurines and other pop culture detritus. Make note of the address; some of the signs aren't easy to see. The trash-to-treasure ratio is higher here than at downtown antique stores, but the finds will probably be cheaper. The flea market has been here forever, and many of the dealers are old-timers who chat companionably with each other over the stalls when things are slow.

S E C R E T
FOLK MUSIC

Since 1981, locals have been heading to **Rasputin's Folk Café** (696 Bronson Avenue, 230-5102, www.cyberus.ca/~rasputin) for folk, blues, Celtic tunes, and other acoustic fare. Rasputin's prides itself on being a performer's place where the audience is there to listen to the music and not just to drink and yell over the tunes. You can't smoke there, but you can drink — Rasputin's is licensed and serves light meals.

The **Black Sheep Inn** (216 River Road, Wakefield, Quebec, 819-459-3228) draws music lovers from all over the Ottawa region for good reason: the place books great bands. It may be located in a pretty country village in the Gatineau Hills, but its entertainment more than competes with anything downtown: Jim Cuddy, Garnet Rogers, Lynn Miles, Tammy Raybould, and many others. Some events are nonsmoking. Come early and chow down in the Temperance Restaurant, enjoy a show, then toddle up to bed in the inn upstairs.

The **Ottawa Folk Festival** (230-8234, www.ottawafolk.org) is a very popular event that attracts crowds to Britannia Park each summer.

SECRET
FONDUE

Just can't get enough of that cheesy 1970s treat? Drop in to the **Fondue Cellar** (Mother Tucker's, 61 York Street, 241-6525). For chocolate dessert fondue, try **Memories** (7 Clarence Street, 241-1882).

SECRET
FORMAL WEAR

Couturier **Richard Robinson** (447 Sussex Drive, 241-5233) has become famous around town because of his most high-profile client, outrageous gal-about-town Marlen Cowpland (wife of high-tech high flyer Michael Cowpland). His dresses for Marlen are regularly splashed across the front pages of the capital's newspapers — the fact that they're usually cut up to here or down to there may have something to do with the news editors' occasional interest in local fashion. However, you don't have to be as out there as Marlen to order a custom-made dress from the designer; he also works with mere mortals. Expect to pay in the four-figure range and to wait at least three weeks for your custom gown.

SECRET
GALLERIES

Art probably isn't the main thing on your mind if you're heading to the **Casino de Hull** (1 Casino Boulevard, Hull, 819-772-2100). However, if you're in the neighbourhood anyway, check out the Canadian artworks hung along Le Promenade du Roi on the third level. In addition, a massive triptych called *L'Hommage à Rosa Luxemburg* dominates the mezzanine. Quebec artist Jean-Paul Riopelle created the dynamic piece.

Another off-the-beaten-track art spot is the **Carleton University Art Gallery** (520-2120, www.carleton.ca/gallery), buried in the basement of St. Patrick's Building on the north end of the campus. Open from noon every day but Monday, it features a regularly changing round of offbeat exhibits. Admission is free.

SECRET
GALLOWS

Although Canada has abolished the death penalty, the gallows in the former Carleton County Gaol — now the **Ottawa International Hostel** (75 Nicholas Street, 235-2595, www.hostellingintl.on.ca) — are still in working condition. They're usually set in motion (with a dummy) once a year, during a Halloween tour of the building. The tour guides used to open them regularly, but pigeons kept flying in and making nests inside them. Contrary to a popular rumour, they're not kept running for the purpose of doing away with anyone convicted of assassinating the queen. By the way, building tours run throughout the year, and they're a fascinating if grisly way to learn about the seedy side of the capital's history.

SECRET
GARDENS

For a place with such wicked winters and such humid summers, Ottawa is buried in gardeners.

The formal garden at **Maplelawn** (529 Richmond Road), a historic mansion built in 1831, was designated a national historic site along with the house in 1989. People just don't make gardens like this one anymore. A substantial limestone wall encloses the garden on three sides, and the riotous displays of peonies and other ornamental perennials were once so famous that bus drivers plying Richmond Road used to slow down so that passengers could gawk at them. In the early 1990s, the garden fell into disrepair, but a group called Friends of Maplelawn Garden has been assiduously rescuing it and restoring it to its former grandeur. The group bases its work on archival records from the 1800s and on plans drawn up by a horticulturist from the Central Experimental Farm who redesigned the garden in 1936. The garden is open to the public and is free of charge — just wander in.

The Ottawa Field-Naturalists Club runs the **Fletcher Wildlife Garden** (off Prince of Wales Drive in the Central Experimental Farm, www.achilles.net/ofnc/fletcher.htm) as a demonstration site to show local homeowners ways to make their yards and other property more friendly to urban wildlife. A trail leading through the seven-hectare site takes you to a butterfly meadow, a rejuvenated woodlot, a living pond, and other wildlife-friendly sites. To get there, follow the signs with the heron logo; the garden is on the east side of Prince of Wales Drive.

Thorne and Co. in the Glebe (802 Bank Street, 232-6565) focuses more on gifts for gardeners than on garden supplies, though it does sell seeds, small tools, and funky pots. But umbrellas, mugs, wrapping paper, and other goodies emblazoned with flowers are the store's real stock in trade.

Quintessential Ottawa (786-1519, www.magma.ca/~ottours/ gardens.html) runs group tours of the greenhouses at Rideau Hall, several private gardens, and the Herb Garden.

I've tried to stay within the borders of urban Ottawa-Hull in this book, but two gardens west of the city in the Ottawa Valley are worth a drive out of town. At the **Herb Garden** (3840 Old Almonte Road, Almonte, Ontario, 613-256-0228, www.herbgarden.on.ca), you can sniff and enjoy some 50 beds of organically grown herbs and other plants and then stop by the gift shop to buy herbal teas, oils, bath products, and gardening gear. And **The Enchanted Gardens** (Beachburg, Ontario, 613-646-2994, www.enchantedgardens.on.ca) include a Japanese garden, an English country garden, a children's playground, and other attractions. Both gardens frequently host weekend workshops on gardening topics.

SECRET
GARLIC

My mouth always starts to water the moment I step into the narrow confines of **The Garlic Gourmet** (1250 Wellington Street, 728-8080, www.thegarlicgourmet.com). Every inch of wall space is stacked with every conceivable garlic concoction, from roasted garlic and sun-dried tomato mustard to honey garlic spice. You'll find garlic pickles, garlic oil, garlic jam, and garlic marinades, as well as clay pots to roast your garlic in and presses to shred it with. A guaranteed vampire-free zone.

If you like your sandwiches *really* garlicky, head to the **Mid-East Food Centre** (1010 Belfast Road, 244-2525) for the cheap pita sandwiches from the deli. Most of them are thickly spread with the most garlicky hummus I've ever encountered. Get a large drink and enjoy. While you're there, browse among the store's eclectic stock, which ranges from bottled lemongrass and Indian curries to pickled lemons and Turkish delight.

SECRET
GAY AND LESBIAN

Ottawa's gay village isn't large or even strictly gay, but it's lively and growing. It stretches along a few blocks of Bank Street between Frank and Lisgar Streets. Shops include a gift and gay erotica shop called **Wilde's** (367 Bank Street, 234-5512), which also draws in a number of straight women with a vast collection of X-rated choco-lates and cards; **One in Ten** (216 Bank Street, 563-0110), which caters to people of all sexual persuasions and sells sex toys and videos; and the self-explanatory **After Stonewall Books** (370 Bank Street, 567-2221).

The **Village Inn Pub** (313 Bank Street, 594-8287) is a casual place that offers all-day breakfasts on weekends. DJs rule the dance floor at the trendy club **Icon** (366 Lisgar Street, 235-4005, www.iconclub.com). The **Centretown Pub** (340 Somerset Street West, 594-0233) is really a collection of bars with something for all tastes. Downstairs is a standard bar with pool tables; upstairs is **Cellblock**, which claims to be Ottawa's only leather and denim cruising bar. A few blocks off Bank Street, **Franky's on Frank** (303 Frank Street, 233-9195) is an exotic dancers' bar with a difference: male dancers for an audience of men.

Just a few blocks from Parliament Hill, in another all-things-to-all-people venture, the **Club Polo Club** (65 Bank Street, 235-5995, www.clubpolo.ottawa.on.ca) features a dance club, a lounge, a rooftop patio, and a wine bar.

In the Byward Market, **The Lookout** (41 York Street, 789-1624) is a casual, second-floor dance club with a great balcony overlooking the market. A few blocks away, **Market Station Bistro** (15 George Street, 562-3540) has a nice patio. And the alternative dance club downstairs, **The Well**, doesn't kid around when it comes to ID — *everyone* is carded at the door.

Ottawa's oldest lesbian bar — in fact, one of the oldest bars in the city — is the **Coral Reef Club** (30 Nicholas Street, 234-5118), which has been in business more than 30 years. It retains a hint of its underground origins: the entrance is hidden away in the Rideau Cen-tre's parking garage. Look for the black door marked discreetly CRC.

On the Quebec side of the Ottawa River, try **Le Pub de la Promenade** (175 Promenade du Portage, Hull, Quebec, 819-771-8810), where the drinks are dirt cheap and the atmosphere is casual. It's not strictly a gay bar, but it's gay friendly.

After a night of partying, you'll need a place to crash. For gay- and lesbian-friendly accommodations, try **Gay Bed & Breakfast** (860-4297) or the **Rideau View Inn** (177 Frank Street, 236-9309).

S E C R E T
G E E K S

OK, before you drive my publisher nuts with angry letters, I want to assure you that I use the term "geeks" with the greatest affection. As the saying goes, some of my best friends are geeks. It's just an easier catchall term than "secret comics, gaming, collectibles, Japanamation," and so forth. With that disclaimer out of the way, let me point you to the stores where you can debate the various merits of D&D versus GURPS or the original *Star Wars* versus *The Phantom Menace* with like-minded souls.

The downtown and west-end branches of **The Comic Book Shoppe** (237 Bank Street, 594-3042, and Bleeker Mall, 1400 Clyde Avenue, 228-8386, www.comicbookshoppe.com) have roughly 1,000 videos for sale or rent. You'll also find Japanamation models and toys, weekly gaming leagues, and comic books. In the Byward Market, **Pagan Playground** (70 George Street, 2nd floor, 241-2227, www.paganplayground.com) has much of the same stuff as well as books on the occult. **Fandom II** (162 Laurier Avenue West, 236-

2972) stocks an extensive supply of role-playing games, books, and miniatures, making it a favourite with many die-hard local gamers. **Silver Snail** (391 Bank Street, 232-2609) has comic books and games as well as toys, magic supplies, and other cool stuff.

SECRET

GERMAN

If you want to eat until you're stuffed, there aren't many better places to do so than **Lindenhof** (965 Richmond Road, 725-3481). The portions of old favourites such as wiener schnitzel are plentiful, and the restaurant is a good source of information on the doings of Ottawa's German Canadian community.

To learn the language itself, try the **Goethe-Institut Ottawa** (480-47 Clarence Street, 241-0273).

SECRET

GHOSTS

Appropriately, the **Haunted Walk of Ottawa** (730-0575, www. hauntedwalk.com) starts its ghost tours from D'Arcy McGee's Pub on Sparks Street, named for an assassinated Victorian politician whose story forms part of the tour. With their black cloaks and lanterns, the guides have become fixtures on Ottawa's nighttime streets. The tours draw many locals as well as tourists, who learn about the ghosts that supposedly walk the halls of the Chateau Laurier, Friday's Roast Beef House, and other downtown establishments.

SECRET
GIFTS

If you need to pick up a unique gift for a wedding or other special occasion, skip most of the overpriced, country-cute shops in the Byward Market. Just a few blocks north of the main market bustle, rent is cheaper, and merchants can take a few more risks. Take **Gizmo Kado** (217 Dalhousie Street, 562-4646). Like most gift stores, it stocks the usual picture frames, vases, dishes, and candles. But you'll find unusual items here that you'll never spot elsewhere.

When the owner of **Ravensara** (1256 Wellington Street, 761-9941) says that many of the teapots, jewellery items, picture frames, soaps, and other items on sale have been made by local artisans, she isn't exaggerating. "Half a dozen of them live in the neighbourhood," she explains. As a result, there are all sorts of unique items here. She does her share by blending her own aromatherapy scents. Try the Blues Buster line; it really is cheering. Most of the nonlocal products are made in Canada.

A few other Ottawa gift shops specialize in Canadian-made items. The two stalwarts are **The Snow Goose** (83 Sparks Street, 232-2213) and **Canada's Four Corners** (93 Sparks Street, 233-2322), both in a touristy area just south of Parliament Hill. They've been around forever and have a good selection of traditional Canadian handicrafts, many of which seem to involve wood, leather, or stone. But if your taste is more modern, try **Snapdragon Fine Crafts** (791 Bank Street, 233-1296), which stocks ceramics, jewellery, hats, and other small goods. I also really like the **Carlen Gallery** (1171 Bank Street, 730-5555), a fascinating place that sells funky jewellery, textiles, paintings, and pottery.

S E C R E T
GOD

The crown jewel of Ottawa's churches has just gone through an extensive restoration, and the results are enough to dazzle even people who hate touring churches. **Notre-Dame Cathedral Basilica** (385 Sussex Drive, 241-7496), built between 1841 and 1853 by the city's French-speaking Catholics, is eye-catching from the outside, particularly the gilded madonna and child atop the front gable, donated in the 1860s by pious lumbermen plying their trade on the Ottawa River below. But the interior is simply mind-boggling. There's no foyer; from the giant front doors, you enter the nave of the church itself. Your eyes won't know where to look first: at the gothic confection of an altar, with 60 or so carved figures of saints surrounding it; at the trompe l'oeil "marble" pillars (they're actually made of wood) with their ornate gold capitals; at the floor, a riot of different red and buff tiles; or at the vivid stained-glass windows. For my money, the best place to look is up, at the vaulted royal blue ceiling spangled with gold stars. It's like walking into an illuminated medieval manuscript. Every visible surface is painted, carved, gilded,

or tiled. This is half church, half theatre, and totally awe-inspiring. The interior originally took more than 40 years to finish, and it shows. Don't miss it.

The oddball exterior, with its unbalanced spires and weird combination of motifs, gives little hint of the gorgeous interior of **St. Brigid's Church** (314 St. Patrick Street, 241-5285). The city has given the complicated woodwork a heritage designation, but the best part of this 1880s Catholic church is the wonderfully light paint job. With its muted pastels and earth tones, it stands out from anything else in Ottawa. The contrast with the over-the-top Notre-Dame is intriguing. It also contrasts with the similar but more exuberant painting at downtown Ottawa's other major Irish church, **St. Patrick's Basilica** (281 Nepean Street, 233-1125).

Deep in the Canadian galleries of the **National Gallery of Canada** (380 Sussex Drive, 990-1985), you'll find the tiny, perfect **Rideau Street Convent Chapel**. Rescued from a local girls' school in 1972 by preservationists, it was dismantled, each piece was carefully numbered, and the whole thing was stored away until 1987, when it was reassembled here. Now deconsecrated, it's frequently the site of classical music concerts. Its delicate fan vaults, cast-iron columns, and other features make it unique in North America. Even empty of furniture and stripped of most of its religious trappings, it's still a peaceful place.

Another reconstructed church in a capital museum is still a house of worship. In the Canada Hall at the **Canadian Museum of Civilization** (100 Laurier Street, Hull, Quebec, 819-776-7000), you can see a complete Ukrainian Catholic church from Smoky Lake, Alberta. At least one couple has tied the knot in this unique wedding venue.

SECRET
GOLF

The Golf Market (855 Industrial Avenue, Unit 12, 247-9212, www.thegolfmarket.net) sells custom clubs and other equipment, but the star attractions are "lake balls": misdirected golf balls that some enterprising soul has fished out of various water traps and recoated. They sell for a quarter of the price of new ones.

If you're fed up with the high green fees and expensive equipment of traditional golf, why not try disc golf? OK, you say, but what is disc golf? It's the same basic game that people have been playing for a long time, except that you use a "flying disc" (a.k.a. "Frisbee") instead of clubs and a ball. You still aim for a "hole" (in this case, a basket on a pole), and you still avoid hazards such as water traps and such. But all you need is a good pair of walking shoes and a Frisbee. The **Ottawa Disc Golf Club** (www.magma.ca/~spratley/discgolf/index.html) is located at Jacques-Cartier Park in Hull. You can borrow discs from the Maison de Vélo (bicycle rental store) in the park. Since the club is a fairly new and totally volunteer operation, the best way to get current information and phone numbers is to go to the web site. Alternatively, you should be able to get basic information at CD **Exchange** (142 Rideau Street, 241-9864), which sells discs for both disc golf and Ultimate Frisbee.

SECRET
GOSPEL

Ottawa isn't exactly known as a gospel hotbed. But you can get your fix every Sunday morning at, of all places, new-wave Italian eatery **Bravo Bravo** (292 Elgin Street, 233-7525), where a gospel group performs during the second and third brunch seatings (noon and 1:30 p.m.). To buy CDs, try **Blessings Christian Marketplace** (5300 Canotek Road, Unit 12, Gloucester, 745-2450), which has a good selection leaning heavily toward recent stuff. Religious radio station **CHRI 99.1 FM** (247-1440, www.chri.ca) beams out several shows featuring gospel music; check the on-line program guide to find out times and dates. Finally, there's usually a rockin' gospel tent at the **Ottawa Bluesfest** every July (233-8798, www.ottawa-bluesfest.ca).

SECRET
GREASY SPOON

Ottawa has an unshakable reputation as a squeaky-clean town, so, needless to say, there isn't much grease on its spoons. But here is one spot to go to satisfy your longings for authentic diner fare.

Mello's (290 Dalhousie Street, 241-1909) is such a Byward Market institution that it's a bit of a cheat to call it a secret. But, as time goes on, the relatively subdued neon glow of Mello's vintage sign gets a little harder to spot amid the relentlessly trendy mishmash of the market. It was known as a hangout for hookers before a big cleanup in the market during the late 1990s forced most of the hookers to less touristy parts of town. But you'll still see the odd high-booted professional woman in here in the wee hours of the morning.

SECRET
GREEK

Craving Greek food but too darned lazy to go out and get it? **Greek on Wheels** (3 Hawthorne Avenue, 235-0056) delivers savory souvlaki and other Greek dishes right to your door. It was a big favourite in the 1999 *Ottawa X Press* readers' poll.

At **Theo's Greek Taverna** (911 Richmond Road, 728-0909, www. theosgreektaverna.com) in the west end, try the trademark tzatziki or the chicken exohiko, an exotic melange of feta cheese, phyllo pastry, and herbs. To wash it down, try one of the Greek wines displayed in racks right at your table or ice-cold Keo beer from Cyprus. On Friday and Saturday nights, a bouzouki band shakes the place up.

The baklava is tooth-achingly sweet, the stuffed grape leaves are luscious, and the waiters are some of the friendliest in town at **Papagus** (281 Kent Street, 233-3626). The ugly, blocky exterior might deter casual passersby, who might mistake the restaurant for an office building, but inside the place is usually jammed and lively.

To give your house or wardrobe a little classical flair, try **Agora** (6 Byward Market, 241-7583, and 801 Bank Street, 565-6414). The

Glebe shop on Bank Street is the bigger of the two, but both stock gilded Greek Orthodox icons, elaborate chess sets, replicas of classical statues and vases, beaded necklaces, and all kinds of leather goods, from sandals to briefcases.

SECRET
GROTTO

One of Ottawa's true oddities, the **Grotte Notre Dame de Lourdes** (435 Montreal Road, 741-4175), is surrounded by apartment buildings and townhouse complexes. Modelled on its namesake in France, it was founded as a local place of pilgrimage in 1871. After moving a few times, it ended up here about 1910. Despite the big signs urging "silence — sanctuary," it isn't very quiet; buses grinding by on nearby Montreal Road and whining lawn mowers from surrounding housing developments cut into the atmosphere somewhat. An artificial grotto of rocks and cement shelters statues of the Virgin Mary, St. Bernadette, and a small altar. A large altar holds pride of place in the front, while a statue of Calvary dominates a small rise of land behind. Green benches provide seating for 600 people. Various plaques, some dating back to 1927, offer thanks for favours received. Not exactly peaceful, but intriguing.

SECRET
HALLS OF FAME

The **Ottawa Sports Hall of Fame** (Ottawa Civic Centre, Lansdowne Park, 1015 Bank Street, 580-2429), founded in 1966, has since inducted more than 170 members. You'll find it in the northwest corner of the arena concourse.

If you thought that the Swiss invented skiing sometime in the 19th century, drop in to the low-key **Canadian Ski Museum** (1960 Scott Street, 722-3584) and learn about 5,000 years of skiing history. The museum is also home to the **Canadian Ski Hall of Fame**. It's free and generally open the same hours as Trailhead, the outdoor shop below it.

SECRET
HATS

People who secretly pine to stun the world with their headgear at England's Ascot races will be in heaven at **Maxine's Designs** (Time Square, 46 Murray Street, 241-5827). The hats on display might include everything from wide-brimmed straw confections festooned with flowers to dainty Jackie Kennedy-style pillboxes and Gatsbyesque cloches, depending on the season. The owner also makes hats to order. A few blocks away, **Chapeaux de Madeleine** (260 St. Patrick Street, 241-8741) and **Eclection** (55 Byward Market, 789-7288) offer hat lovers more choices.

SECRET
HEALTH CLUBS

Inexpensive day passes will get you in at several downtown gyms, including the **Metro Central Y** (180 Argyle Street, 788-5000) and the **Downtown Y Centre** (99 Bank Street, 233-9331). You can also get a day pass to the tony club at the **Chateau Laurier** (1 Rideau Street, 241-1414), with its elegant Edwardian pool.

SECRET
HERALDRY

Some rich families seem to have all the luck. Not only are they rolling in dough, but those with old European roots have a family coat of arms that they can hang above the manorial fireplace. You may not be able to get into that swanky country club or snooty wine-tasting society that you've been fantasizing about, but you can ask the Canadian government for your own coat of arms.

Canadians used to have to go cap in hand back to the mother country to get an official shield-and-fierce-animals logo. But in 1988 Queen Elizabeth II gave Canada the right to create its own. The **Canadian Heraldic Authority** (www.gg.ca/herald_e.html, and heavens no, dear, you can't *phone*) now falls under the governor general's wing. The Canadian Space Agency, Corel Corporation, and various politicians have been among the 100 or so applicants for a coat of arms each year. To join them, all you need is $1,500 to $3,000 to pay for the research and artwork. If this sounds like your cup of tea, send your request to the Chief Herald of Canada, Canadian Heraldic Authority, Rideau Hall, Ottawa, Ontario, KIA OAI. Don't forget to provide the reasons why you or your company deserves such a goodie.

If your background is Irish, there's a good chance that **O'Shea's Market Ireland** (91 Sparks Street, 235-5141, www.osheasmarket ireland.com) can make a T-shirt, sweatshirt, or baseball cap with your name on it. The store has more than 600 Celtic coats of arms in its database, from Adam to Young. O'Shea's also sells Aran sweaters, Irish music, walking sticks, claddagh rings, and other memorabilia of the ould sod. Scots, on the other hand, may want to hie themselves to **House of Scotland** (759-8232, call first for hours).

SECRET
HIDDEN
RESTAURANTS

Café Joompa (192 chemin de la Colonie, Vals-des-Monts, Quebec, 819-457-9508) is the sort of place that you'd never find by accident. I know about it only because a friend who lives nearby generously shared information about her area's best-kept secret. About a half-hour drive from downtown Ottawa, Café Joompa is housed on the first floor of a two-storey, 4,500-square-foot "cottage" in the Gatineau Hills. The owners live upstairs and serve Malaysian Canadian cuisine downstairs in what used to be the living room. The table d'hôte menu (choose from two starters, three mains, and two desserts) changes monthly and might include chicken satay, slowly braised lamb shanks, seared ostrich salad, or eggplant–sweet potato curry. As befits a place based in a cottage, the restaurant has a casual ambience (though diners often dress up). Patrons can stroll out to the rock garden and relax in the hammock between courses. Some spend the whole dinner outside on the terrace, next to the cascading stream. The only iron-clad rule is that you must phone ahead for reservations; if the restaurant doesn't have enough reservations, it won't open on a given night. Summer Saturday nights and special-event dinners such as Valentine's Day are often booked solid. So, if you're flexible about dates and don't mind planning ahead, do try it. And, since Café Joompa is licensed to serve wine but not to sell it, bring your own bottle.

I'd never heard of the **Capital Club** (Delta Ottawa Hotel, 361 Queen Street, 238-6000) until my father-in-law took us to dinner there recently for my birthday. Then, the next week, someone suggested the restaurant through the Secret Cities web site. So maybe this hidden gem is about to start drawing crowds. Get there quickly before it does. A tiny, elegant room with the feel of a private gentlemen's club — high-backed chairs, quiet classical music, and plenty of dark wood — it serves superb continental cuisine. This is the sort of place where dishes artfully decorated with towers of fresh herbs are hidden under domed covers until they can be revealed with a flourish. Unlike some such places, particularly those located in hotels, the food is fantastic, and the waiters are friendly, efficient, and totally unpretentious. Since there are only about 10 tables, reservations are essential.

Most people who drop in to **The French Baker** (119 Murray Street, 789-7941) pick up their baguettes or croissants (see Secret Croissants) and go on their merry way without suspecting that a restaurant lies hidden at the end of a long hallway at the back of the shop. Follow that corridor and you'll come to an eye-catching space where each wall is painted a different primary colour, with the whole thing somehow harmonized by a checkerboard black-and-white floor. Place your order at the counter. You can nosh at one of the half-dozen tables or get takeout. The light menu changes daily and usually includes at least one fish, one chicken, and one vegetarian dish, such as poached salmon, couscous, or paella.

SECRET
HOCKEY

Of course, the Ottawa Senators get most of the attention. After all, they're the guys with the big paycheques, the big advertising budgets, and the big Stanley Cup hopes. But along with all that, they also have big ticket prices.

For a cheaper, less commercialized night at the rink, my vote is with the junior league **Ottawa 67s** (www.ottawa67s.com). This Ontario Hockey Association team brought home the Memorial Cup in 1984 and 1999. They've been here longer than their overhyped colleagues across town, and they have a devoted following. As well they should: for just $10 (and as little as $6.50 per child), you can watch a great game of fast-paced hockey. And, when the night is done, you don't have to spend another hour fighting your way out of the parking lot, only to find yourself somewhere west of Kanata when you finally escape.

SECRET
HOUSEWARES

Stainless steel cookware, cutlery, appliances, and bowls are the name of the game at **The Cookware Centre** (220 Bank Street, 235-6020), which has been at this location since 1965. Owner Wilfred Finn started the business four years earlier, selling pots and pans door to door. These days, his children largely run the store, and the young couples coming in to equip their first homes are likely to be the grandchildren of Finn's early, loyal clients. As well as his trademark Vitality II line of cookware, he buys overstocks, end-of-the-lines, and inventory from liquidators, so there's always a good chance of finding, well, a "steel."

The **Paderno Factory Store** inside the Glebe Emporium (724 Bank Street, 567-2205 or 233-3474, www.paderno.com) is worth a visit if you're a serious amateur (or professional) gourmet. This is one of several outlets across the country for the Prince Edward Island company that makes high-end Paderno and Chaudier cookware. You can pick up top-quality pieces at 40% off the retail price and seconds at 50% off. Chaudier is the more expensive line, designed for restaurants, cooking schools, and gourmets. Neither line is exactly cheap, but if you want cheap items don't come to the Glebe.

Domus is the mother of all Ottawa cookware shops. Although the selection here seems to have shrunk somewhat since the store moved from its previous location on Dalhousie Street, there's still a lot to see. Domus is aimed at the home cook who can't imagine life without a spaetzle maker, an herb mill, or an asparagus steamer. On any given weekend, the aisles are clogged with amateur gourmets rifling through

shelves of Le Creuset cookware, linen aprons, lemon zesters, and British teapots. For those with nonstratospheric budgets, there are usually good deals on the scratch-and-dent shelf at the back, such as funky coffee mugs with slightly chipped bases for just one dollar. And even though the prices aren't cheap, the stuff is generally good. The nifty Swiss corkscrew that I picked up here years ago (on sale for half price) is indestructible, and, even though it looks like a medical instrument from *Star Trek*, it works well.

Around the corner, strangely enough, a similar cookware store moved into the premises that Domus vacated. For some reason, though, **Ma Cuisine** (269 Dalhousie Street, 789-9225) isn't as much of a yuppie temple as its older competitor. Sure, there's boomer loot galore here, such as Emile Henry casserole dishes and picnic backpacks, but the prices aren't as high, and the gizmos aren't as esoteric.

SECRET
ICE CREAM

Sadly, outstanding ice cream is hard to find in the capital these days. I used to be a rabid fan of **Lois 'n' Frima's** (several locations) product, but although it's good it isn't superb anymore. Similarly, **Cows** (43 Clarence Street, 244-4224) has its fans, but those who've tasted the ice cream from the original Cows outlet in Prince Edward Island say that the local stuff doesn't compare.

So what's an ice-cream lover to do? There's always gelato, and the reigning king in this field is **Piccolo Grande** (55 Murray Street, 241-2909, and 413 MacKay Street, 747-1565). Its Italian-style ices are good but expensive. For about the same price as a kiddie cup at Piccolo Grande, you can get a full-sized, one-scoop cone of sweet, smooth gelato at **Pasticceria Gelateria Italiana** (200 Preston Street, 233-2104), where you can also pig out on fantastic pastries by award-winning chefs.

S E C R E T
INDIAN

Indian restaurants are hugely popular in Ottawa, and choosing among them is difficult. For its elegant ambience alone, I like **Café Shafali** (308 Dalhousie, 789-9188). **Light of India** (730 Bank Street, 563-4411) makes the best kashmiri chicken and nan I've discovered in Ottawa, while the butter chicken at **Roses Café** (523 Gladstone, 233-5574, and two other locations) is probably what God himself orders for takeout.

The "dinner Kohinoor" for two at **Mukut Restaurant** (610 Rideau Street, 789-2220) is a great deal: shami kabab, onion bhaji, tandoori chicken, beef curry, aloo peas, palao rice, nan, pappadum, and gulab jammun for under $35. I defy two people to polish off the whole tasty thing without asking for a doggy bag. Better yet, get takeout, since the ornate carved chairs are devilishly uncomfortable. By the end of a long, leisurely meal, you'll feel both satisfied and stiff.

SECRET
INSPIRATIONAL
MESSAGES

If you're driving down Elgin Street, watch for the notice board in front of **St. John the Evangelist Anglican Church** (154 Somerset Street West, 232-4500), at the corner of Elgin and Somerset Streets. Rector Garth Bulmer has been collecting thought-provoking sayings and posting them on the board for years; sometimes parishioners give him suggestions. They all have a philosophical or religious slant, but you're more likely to see some keen but little-known observation from Henry David Thoreau or Simone Weil than you are to catch one of the more famous phrases from St. Paul. The messages, which never fail to make me stop and think, are changed regularly.

SECRET
INUIT

The annual **Inuit Qaggiq** is an annual spring festival of Inuit art and culture. For dates and locations, contact the Inuit Art Foundation (2081 Merivale Road, Nepean, 224-8189). It shares space with the **Inuit Artists' Shop**, which also has a store in the Byward Market (16 Clarence Street, 241-9444). Across the street in the market, **Northern Country Arts** (21 Clarence Street, 789-9591) also sells Inuit artworks.

S E C R E T
IRISH

The Irish have been prominent in Ottawa since Irish labourers helped to build the Rideau Canal. Today you can drop in to at least half a dozen fairly good Irish-style pubs around the city. **D'Arcy McGee's** (44 Sparks Street, 230-4433) is named for the unfortunate Irish Canadian politician who met his fate in Canada's first political assassination two blocks down the street. On Thursday and Friday nights, in particular, it's often full of rambunctious office workers and hill staffers easing the work week's cares away with a pint or two of Guinness.

Can't make it to the Abbey Theatre? Try Ottawa's **Tara Players** (St. Patrick's Hall, 280 Gloucester Street, 746-1410, www.ncf.ca/taraplayers), a community theatre troupe that performs primarily Irish plays by writers such as Brian Friel, John Millington Synge, and William Butler Yeats. Sure, the aging church hall isn't exactly the National Arts Centre, but the spirit of community theatre is infectious here. The company was founded in 1976 by a group of Hibernophiles and Irish ex-pats. It had an enormous wave of success in the early 1990s, when it won the nationwide Theatre Canada festival and took its production of Friel's play *Freedom of the City* to an international competition in Ireland. I have to admit my bias here: I was a member of Tara for many years (until my travel and work commitments made it difficult to contribute much) and remember it with great affection. The same hall also plays host to monthly ceilis (music nights) and to weekly music lessons and dance classes, organized by the Ottawa branch of **Comhaltas Ceoltóiri Éireann** (www.acs.ucalgary.ca/~bmccombs/comhaltas/Ottawa). Comhaltas (pronounced "Coltas") is an international Irish cultural organization.

SECRET
ITALIAN

Most of Ottawa's Little Italy is clustered around Preston and Gladstone Streets. But go a bit farther south on Preston, toward Carling Avenue, and you'll stumble on **Restorante Il Piccolino** (449 Preston Street, 236-8158). In the summer, head for the intimate, vine-shrouded terrace to linger over well-priced pasta and meat specialties and indulge in a bottle or two from the wide-ranging wine list.

The ultratrendy **Bottega Nicastro Fine Food Shop** (64 George Street, 789-7575) in the Byward Market caters to the stylish gourmet. However, for one of the best selections of Italian staples in the city, head to its mother ship in the suburbs, **Nicastro's** (1558 Merivale Road, Nepean, 225-3470). There you can buy pasta in just about any shape and olive oil in just about every condition of virginity.

SECRET
JAPANESE

Want to throw an elaborate Japanese dinner or tea ceremony? Get your supplies at **East Wind** (794 Bank Street, 567-0382), a Glebe fixture that sells high-quality teapots, chopsticks, noodle bowls, and other tableware. Creative types can buy calligraphy equipment and rice paper for authentic invitations. Feng shui books, kimono, and other Eastern goods round out the stock. In the west end, **Pack Rabbit** (see Secret Prints) stocks similar products.

On a terrace near Les Muses restaurant at the **Canadian Museum of Civilization** (100 Laurier Street, Hull, Quebec, 819-776-7000) is an oasis that I'd never heard of until a friend told me about it: a traditional Japanese Zen garden. According to him, the best time to visit it is after a rain, when it sparkles. Not your typical green garden, it's a dry-features garden where every stone tells a story on the theme of *wakei no niwa* (respect for other cultures). The centrepiece is a stone waterfall and a stretch of dry, raked gravel resembling a stream, which symbolize the influence of Japanese culture. Landscape architect and Zen Buddhist monk Shunmyo Toshiaki Masuno designed the garden using local stones. Funded by a Japanese foundation, the garden was built in the mid-1990s.

The **Fulford Gallery** (75 Hinton Avenue North, 722-0440, www. cyberus.ca/~fulford) specializes in antique prints, etchings, and maps. Along with European and North American pieces, however, you'll find a collection of 19th-century Japanese woodblock prints, starting around $30.

OK, so it isn't precisely a Japanese restaurant. I didn't know where else to put **Hino** (1013 Wellington Street, 722-1129). An unusual eatery that doesn't fit neatly into any category, it attracts food lovers from around the city to a very nontrendy stretch of Wellington. Many of the dishes have Japanese roots, but you can also find pasta, curries, Californian cuisine, and other surprises on the menu.

SECRET
JAZZ

The **Ottawa International Jazz Festival** (July, Confederation Park and other locations, 241-2633, www.jazz.ottawa.com) itself isn't much of a secret. But here's one: if someone major is playing, and you suspect that Confederation Park is going to be jammed, come early and grab a spot on the nearby Laurier Bridge. You'll have to stand, and the view and acoustics aren't as good as in the park itself, but you'll make a quick getaway. And you'll be able to enjoy the show for free.

SECRET
JEWELLERY

Planning to pop the big question? You don't have to settle for a mass-produced engagement ring. Several jewellers around town do innovative custom work. Try **Hutchings and Cremin** (55 Murray Street, 241-2266), **Somerset Villiage Goldsmiths and Artisans** (100-346 Somerset Street West, 234-5969), or **Goldform Manufacturing Jewellers** (161 Holland Avenue, 725-2210).

SECRET
JUDAICA

In the early 1930s, a Montreal businessman began amassing a library of rare Jewish and Hebrew books. Four decades later, he donated it to the National Library of Canada, where the **Jacob M. Lowy Collection** (395 Wellington Street, 995-7960, www.nlc-bnc.ca/services/elowy.htm) is now Canada's best collection of such materials and one of the most important collections of rare Judaica in the world. Housed on the second floor, it includes some 3,000 rare books and 1,500 related items, such as encyclopedias, exhibition catalogues, and dictionaries. And, remarkably, it is open to the public — just call the curator from the desk in the library's main lobby and ask for admittance (someone will come down to escort you). You may find yourself staring at the first scientific book ever printed in Hebrew, an early example of secular Jewish poetry, or a first edition of the King James Bible. There are more than 40 15th-century volumes in the collection, including the National Library's oldest book, a Latin edition of *The Jewish Antiquities* from 1470.

SECRET
KARAOKE

Madonna wannabes should head to **Granata Music** (1558 Merivale Road, Nepean, 727-0727) for one of the city's largest selections of karaoke tapes, including belt-'em-out favourites such as Elvis Presley,

Billy Joel, and Clint Black. There's Anne Murray for those of a milder disposition and *The Lion King* soundtrack for the kiddies. To rent a machine for a raucous home party, try **A Sharp Singalong Karaoke** (21-1010 Polytek Road, Gloucester, 741-2574) or **All Canadian Karaoke and DJ** (824-8499). The former also sells karaoke machines, as does **Radio Shack** (286 Bank Street, 238-6889, and numerous other locations). However, if nothing will do but making a fool of yourself in public, call the **Karaoke Hotline** (745-7337) or the **Karaoke Info Hotline** (824-4137) to find out which bars and restaurants are featuring open-mike nights. *Volare!*

S E C R E T

LATIN AMERICAN

Perhaps people back from vacation dream of re-creating their holidays at home. Or maybe sun-starved Ottawans will try anything to imagine themselves out of a brutal northern winter. Whatever the reason, Latin American furniture and decor stores have suddenly started to proliferate in the nation's capital.

Polanco (109 Clarence Street, 562-0782) specializes in massive articles of Mexican pine furniture as well as glassware, mirrors, wrought-iron candelabra, and clay pots. A few blocks away, Julia Enriquez and her husband, Ivan Dellaire, opened **Mexican Treasures** (211 Dalhousie Street, 562-9495) in May 2000. The bright little shop sells small decorative items such as crystal, paintings, picture frames, silver jewellery, ceramics, linens, and lamps. The couple travel to Mexico two or three times a year to check out new products, and everything in the shop is handmade and imported. In Ottawa South, **Casa Luna** (1115 Bank Street, 730-3561) is almost a vacation in itself. Latin American music — no doubt chosen by shop co-owner Alex Grooscors, host of the *Barrio Latino* program on CKCU-FM — pours softly out of hidden speakers. Solid tables inlaid with intricate tiles are set with gaily patterned dishes, while vivid Chilean paintings brighten the walls.

If your budget or luggage space doesn't run to large tables and armoires, try **True South** (827 Bank Street, 233-2026) for woven bags from Guatemala and wooden toys from El Salvador as well as items from other southern locales, such as batiks from the Philippines. Just down the street, **Quichua Crafts** (799 Bank Street, 567-7767; also 175 Sparks Street, 594-4836; www.quichuacrafts.com) has more of an Andean accent, with panpipes and South American CDs as well as jewellery, cotton clothes, and bright ceramics.

SECRET
LAUNDROMATS

If you get bored doing your laundry (and who doesn't?), there's always **Wringers** (151 Second Avenue, 234-9700). While your undies go through the spin cycle, you can knock back a drink at the bar, have a sandwich, or play a game of pool. The place even takes credit cards.

SECRET
LEBANESE

Ottawa has a large, vibrant Lebanese Canadian community. Before I moved here, I had never heard of shawarma or falafel; now you can pick up these and other Middle Eastern munchies almost everywhere. As well as the ubiquitous takeout places, there are at least two top-notch, upscale Lebanese restaurants in town: **Fairouz** (343 Somerset Street West, 233-1536) and **Kamals** (787 Bank Street, 234-5223). For something a bit less ritzy, try the **Glebe Café** (840 Bank Street, 235-1289). It's dressed itself up a bit in recent years, with multicoloured rugs on the walls and other Middle Eastern touches. But it's kept the great vintage movie posters and the reasonable prices that I remember from my student days at nearby Carleton University. It's a great place to meet a friend for a long, gossipy lunch.

SECRET
LIBRARIES

The library at the **National Gallery of Canada** (380 Sussex Drive, 998-8949) is Canada's largest collection of books and resources about the visual arts, and it's open to the public. The hours are fairly restricted, though, so call ahead. It's a good idea to phone ahead in any case, since some of the books are stored offsite, and it may take a day or two to get them to the gallery. You'll have many to choose from, since the collection includes 230,000 books, exhibition catalogues, and bound periodicals, 41,000 auction catalogues, and 182,000 slides. The gallery even provides an elegant setting for your research: a sunny third-floor room with big windows overlooking the Ottawa River, with large tables lit by stylish black banker's lamps.

St. Paul University (223 Main Street, 236-1393), a bilingual theological school that evolved from the University of Ottawa, is home to Canada's largest library of philosophy, theology, and medieval studies, with more than 400,000 books alone, as well as all kinds of periodicals, CD-ROMs, and other materials. Since the university started as a Roman Catholic seminary and has a long association with the Oblates of Mary Immaculate, the collection of Roman Catholic texts and works on canon law is particularly large. But the library also has resources related to all Christian denominations, particularly the Anglican and Eastern Orthodox churches. The library buys works in German, Italian, Spanish, Portuguese, Dutch, Latin, Greek, Hebrew, English, and French; it also houses some books in Polish, Ukrainian, and Russian that it has received as gifts. Members of the public are welcome to use the library but should call first for information on access.

SECRET
LINGERIE

Don't be put off by the signs all over the parking lot warning you that "These Premises Are Under Camera Surveillance." A visit to **Warner's Factory Outlet** (2355 St. Laurent Boulevard, 737-0563) is worth running the unusual security gauntlet. With Fruit of the Loom bras for three dollars and Calvin Klein T-shirts for nine dollars, what's not to love? Go on a weekday if you'd like to browse in peace; on the weekends, there are often sales, and from all reports the place turns into a war zone of bargain-crazed women scuffling for the last ostrich-feathered Marilyn Monroe bra.

If you have silk tastes on a polyester budget, another good stop is **Silkwear** (951 Gladstone Avenue, 722-6838) for samples and overruns of silk camisoles, nightgowns, and pajamas on sale for about half the suggested retail price. Don't worry if no one's there when you open the door; someone will pop out soon from behind the curtain that separates the small shop from the sewing room next door.

SECRET
MACKENZIE KING

As far as I can tell, William Lyon Mackenzie King was one of the most offbeat guys ever to make it to the prime minister's office, and he still holds the record for having served longer than anyone else. But he had a few, shall we say, quirks.

Granted, he did leave his country home in the Gatineau Hills, Moorside, to the nation. It is now a museum of his life, the **Mackenzie King Estate** (Kingsmere Road, Gatineau Park, Quebec, 819-827-2020), in the heart of Gatineau Park. But he also decorated the grounds of said estate with all sorts of ersatz "ruins," such as bits of the British Bank of North America, demolished in Ottawa in 1936, and fragments of the original Parliament buildings. He even asked

Lester Pearson, then a diplomat at Canada House in London, to send him some bombed bits of the Palace of Westminster during the Second World War. Pearson, miraculously, complied; the pieces were sent back to Canada by submarine. The ruins are a pretty place to take photos today.

King seems to have been a man of strong likes and dislikes, and he wasn't shy about immortalizing people whom he admired. Right in front of Parliament Hill, a charming statue of a young man dressed as Sir Galahad holds pride of place. The plaque below tells part of the story: it's a memorial to **Henry Albert Harper**, a 28-year-old man who died trying to save a woman who'd fallen through the ice in the Ottawa River during a skating party in 1901. What it doesn't reveal is that Harper was King's best friend and that the heartbroken King organized the subscription drive himself. Almost two decades later, when local poet **William Campbell** died, King led the drive to build a memorial bench beside Campbell's grave in Beechwood Cemetery. A few lines from a Campbell poem are carved on one end, and there's a bronze likeness of the poet. King wanted the bench to give fellow admirers of this now forgotten poet a place to relax and ponder his work.

King also had a lifelong interest in spiritualism. Today, in his restored study at **Laurier House** (335 Laurier Avenue East, 992-8142), you can see the crystal ball that he once received as a gift. The guides say that he used it only once or twice, but I think that a man known for his strong attachment to his deceased mother and dog must have been tempted to try it out a few times.

SECRET
MALAYSIAN

Chahaya Malaysia (1690 Montreal Road, Gloucester, 742-0242) has a long reputation for fiery food. It's the kind of place where many people order simply by giving numbers of dishes on the menu. Years ago, I went to the old location in the Glebe with a group of people from the newspaper where I worked. My editor boasted that he could handle food as hot as they could make it; after a long, fabulous meal of watery eyes, he gasped that we should make up T-shirts declaring "I survived number 27 at Chahaya Malaysia." Not all the food is smoking, though; the chef takes pity on those with timid taste buds with mild dishes such as grilled beef kajang.

SECRET
MANSIONS

There's no house in town that even comes close in terms of price. Assessed for tax purposes at more than $9 million, the 20,000-square-foot home of **Michael and Marlen Cowpland** (Soper Place, Rockcliffe Park) attracts a steady stream of rubbernecks. Cowpland, founder of local software giant Corel Corporation, has built a rambling house of mirrored glass and copper-coloured accents that looks more like an office building than a private home. If you do drive up there, you'll also have the chance to snoop around one of the ritziest sections of the village. Around the corner is the **Apostolic**

Nunciature (724 Manor Avenue), home of the pope's representative in Canada. It's a huge structure reminiscent of an English lord's estate, and you can glimpse it through the arched gate. The oldest part of the mansion dates back to 1835. A few blocks away and a century younger, the residence of the **Ambassador of Japan** (725 Acacia Avenue) has a similar baronial look. It was originally built for one of the heirs to the Bronson lumber fortune.

S E C R E T
MAPS

A World of Maps (1235 Wellington Street, 724-6776, www.worldof maps.com) sells city, provincial, state, country, hiking, topographical, and just about any other kind of map you can think of as well as tourist guidebooks and map-related materials (such as envelopes made from disused maps). For anyone interested in either geography or travel, it's an oddly compelling place. And if you like it you'll probably enjoy **Place Bell Books** (175 Metcalfe Street, 233-3821, www. cyberus.ca/~pbb/main.html). There the emphasis is more on travel guides, but there's also a decent selection of international maps for major tourist hotspots, particularly in the United States and Europe.

Federal Maps Inc. (52 Antares Drive, Unit 1, Nepean, 723-6366, www.fedmaps.com) is Canada's largest regional distributor of maps and charts produced by the federal Canada Map Office. This is where map dealers across Ontario come to get their stock, but the company also sells maps directly to the public.

If antique maps are more your speed, the **Astrolabe Gallery** (71 Sparks Street, 234-2348) buys and sells old maps from the 15th through the 19th centuries. There's also a fun selection of antique prints and posters.

SECRET
MARTINIS

The funky martini craze shows no signs of abating, in Ottawa at least. Two of the most stylish places to make like James Bond are located, not surprisingly, in the Byward Market. For ages, I was convinced that the **Empire Grill** (47 Clarence Street, 241-1343) was actually called the Manhattan Grill, probably because its Art Deco style and cooler than cool crowd made me think of New York. This place to see and be seen is part restaurant, part club, and all attitude. The food is a mix of New American cuisine and traditional steakhouse fare. And, in addition to more than a dozen martinis, there's a large wine menu.

Meanwhile, a few blocks away, the **Mercury Lounge** (56 Byward Market, 789-5324) is so cutting-edge that I find it hard to believe it's even in Ottawa. You climb up a narrow staircase and suddenly find yourself in an airy, two-storey bar with a massive red-brick wall, huge windows swathed in luxurious drapes, a long bar serving up more types of martinis than I can count, and an elegant mezzanine. It draws a mid-20s crowd to listen and lounge to the latest tunes, and it is just too cool for words. (Granted, by the time that this book comes out, both places may just be "so five minutes ago." That's how it goes when you're a trendsetter.)

SECRET
MAZES

Saunders Farm (Munster, 838-5440, www.saundersfarm.com, open to the public in October only), about half an hour from downtown Ottawa, is a great family attraction that offers haunted Halloween parties and other kid-friendly activities. But the most unusual attractions are the six hedge mazes, begun in the early 1990s. The humdinger is the enormous Mile Maze, which the owners warn is "not for the impatient or lazy." The Cedar Hedge Maze, with its seven-foot trees, was inspired by a maze at the Zurich airport; the trees in the Spiral Maze are just three feet tall, making this one less intimidating for kids. If you get to the end of the Spruce Hedge Maze, you can climb up to a two-storey tree fort. Finally, the Grapevine Maze is a particularly twisted labyrinth.

SECRET
MEDITATION

The **Shambhala Meditation Centre** (982 Wellington Street, 725-9321) regularly offers free instruction. There are also introductory sessions in Christian meditation at **St. Patrick's Basilica** (277 Nepean Street entrance, 236-9437). The **Joyful Land Buddhist Centre** (562 Somerset Street West, 234-4347, www.sona.ca/~joyfulland) offers a bewildering variety of classes.

SECRET
MEMORABILIA

I had a terrible time trying to find a heading to classify **Straight 'n' Wicked** (1167 Bank Street, 730-9494). First I tried "Secret Hawaiian" because the store stocks an amazing selection of rayon Hawaiian shirts, flowered dresses, and silk leis. But then I thought about the selection of bowling shirts and tie-dyed shirts and thought "Secret Retro" might be better. All the South Park, Beatles, and radio-station-logo clothes brought to mind "Secret Pop Culture." But the clincher was store-owner "Uncle Bob" Cabana's collection of rock star autographs and other flotsam and jetsam. He buys, sells, and trades, so come in and ask what's available: a signed copy of John Lennon's book *In His Own Write*, a GI Joe lunchbox, Al Pacino's autograph, Corgi toy cars, a tambourine signed by Emerson, Lake, and Palmer — you name it, Uncle Bob might have it, if he hasn't sold it already. Call ahead to find out what's in stock.

Also in the memorabilia field, **Elgin Street Video** (258-A Elgin Street, 236-1877) is known for its window displays of movie props, scripts, costumes, and other memorabilia. Most of the pieces are for sale, such as the authentic Jimmy Stewart autograph that my husband once bowled me over with on my birthday. And, of course, the store also rents videos. While you'll find all the latest Hollywood blockbusters, there's also a formidable collection of classics, foreign films, gay movies, and videos of British TV series. You can wallow in elegant Cary Grant comedies, Second World War weepies, over-the-top MGM musicals, 1950s westerns, French New Wave flicks, creepy 1970s cult movies, and all the other movies you (or your grandparents) had half forgotten.

S E C R E T
MILITARY

The Governor General's Foot Guards are one of two regiments of red-coated soldiers who carry out the Changing the Guard ceremony each summer morning on Parliament Hill. Since 1882, they've called the **Cartier Square Drill Hall** (Cartier Square, 2 Queen Elizabeth Drive) home, making the building the oldest continuously operating drill hall in Canada. The hall was restored in the 1990s and is home to two small military museums: one for the Governor General's Foot Guards themselves and one for the Cameron Highlanders of Ottawa.

Confederation Park (Elgin Street at Laurier Avenue West) is home to an eclectic collection of military memorials. The soldier gallantly doffing his hat is the **Boer War Memorial**, a 1902 monument paid for by donations of pennies from 30,000 schoolchildren. Elsewhere in the park, the sculpture of two sombre soldiers in bearskin hats, the **Northwest Rebellion Monument**, commemorates two members of the Governor General's Foot Guards killed in 1885 during the Riel Rebellion. The park is also home to the **Polish Home Army Tribute**, a plaque paying tribute to 26 Canadian airmen killed during the Second World War in Poland.

The military monument with the most scenic location is probably the **Commonwealth Air Force Memorial** (Sussex Drive, near the French Embassy). The stylized globe commemorates the 800 fliers who perished in Canada during the Second World War (most were killed during training flights or while ferrying planes overseas). It's located in a small park near the point where the Rideau River tumbles over a small cliff into the Ottawa River at Rideau Falls.

S E C R E T
MINGLING

The organizers at the National Gallery of Canada (990-1985) are loath to call their **After Hours** series a singles program because the elegant evenings attract a mixed artsy crowd of all ages, including couples. Most of the events include an introduction to a major exhibition or collection at the gallery as well as hors d'oeuvres, a wine tasting, or some other high-class food event.

S E C R E T
MONEY

Money may not grow on trees, but it once came on playing cards. The **Currency Museum** (245 Sparks Street, 782-8914, www.bank-banque-canada.ca) has playing-card money from revolutionary France, a handwritten 10-pound note from Glorious Revolution-era England, a Chinese woodblock note from 1368, and POW scrip from the Second World War. There are also more coins than you can count as well as many other items once used as money: glass beads, bone necklaces, seashells, and fur pelts. It's all strangely fascinating. The museum is free and often half deserted.

In one of Ottawa's more interesting urban legends, the largest gold deposit in the world is supposedly located in the Bank of Canada vaults under Wellington Street. The public relations people at the bank assured me that this was a myth, and it does seem to be highly unlikely, since we've been off the gold standard for years. But do you think they'd tell a lowly writer where the nation's loot is hidden? Conspiracy theorists, pack your metal detectors.

SECRET
MOUNTIES

If you want to get your picture taken with a Mountie in full dress, complete with red serge jacket and high boots, go to Parliament Hill on any summer day. Two Mounties are usually on duty, unless it's pouring rain or a special event is taking place. The horses are brought in each morning and stabled in a small area behind the National Capital Commission's Info-Tent when they're not on duty.

But to get the whole story behind the Mounties, their steeds, and the famous Musical Ride, go to the **RCMP Musical Ride Centre** (RCMP Rockcliffe Stables, Sandridge Road at St. Laurent Boulevard, 993-3751, www.rcmp-grc.gc.ca/frames/rcmp-grc1.htm). There you can find out more about how the horses are bred and trained, watch a blacksmith at work, see the carriages that the queen uses when she's in town, and learn a lot about the history of the force. To get a close look at the horses grazing, drive along the Rockcliffe Parkway and park in the small lot near the stables. I've never tried this, but evidently a bag full of carrots will make you the most popular guest in the pasture.

SECRET
MOVIES

I first saw *Casablanca*, and many other classic movies, on the big screen at the **Mayfair Theatre** (1074 Bank Street, 730-3403, www.mayfair-movie.com). This venerable repertory house first opened for business on December 5, 1932, as a first-run cinema, complete with phony balconies and lots of red plush. Since then, it's been drawing in budget-conscious students from nearby Carleton University and movie fans from across the city with cheap double bills. The schedule balances old classics, cult films (*Rocky Horror*, anyone?), and popular foreign movies with plenty of recent Hollywood hits. In the winter, buy your ticket early and then head to the pub next door, the unfortunately named **Mad Cow**, to keep warm; there's not much of a lobby at the Mayfair, and you may find yourself lined up outside if you're not careful.

A similar problem exists at Ottawa's other repertory theatre, the artsier **Bytowne Cinema** (325 Rideau Street, 789-FILM, www.ottawa.film-can.com/). Built in 1947, the building was a first-run cinema for 40 years until Famous Players sold it to the owners of the Towne Cinema, an art house that had held sway on the corner of Beechwood Avenue and Crichton Street since 1973. The Towne moved a couple of miles closer to downtown and became the Bytowne. More avant-garde than the Mayfair, it features a heavier proportion of subtitled, risky, and obscure films. Don't miss the yummy baked goods and herbal tea at the snack bar. And, to avoid cold toes in the winter, grab a quick meal at the tiny **Vietnamese Noodle House** next door or at **Nate's Deli** across the street while waiting for the Bytowne's doors to open.

For more than 20 years, families have been enjoying kid-friendly flicks at the **West End Family Cinema** (Notre Dame Auditorium, 170 Broadview Avenue, 722-8218, www.familycinema.org). The movies are relatively current, and the prices can't be beat: individual admissions start at just two dollars, and the chips, chocolate bars, and pop at the snack bar are a dollar each. Added perks include a big screen, digital sound, free parking, and party nights. A registered charity, the cinema screens movies each Saturday afternoon and every second Friday night from September to May (except at Christmas and Easter).

So you're convinced that the only way you're going to see a movie that you love is to write, direct, produce, and star in it yourself. Unfortunately, your experience with filmmaking is limited to a few weekends at the cottage monkeying around with your brother-in-law's video camera. Sounds like you need the **Canadian Screen Training Centre** (789-4720, www.cstc.ca), which offers a variety of courses in screenwriting, directing, and other movie skills throughout the year. The highlight of the program is the Summer Institute of Film and Television, a six-day event each June that brings in big names such as Anthony Minghella (director of *The English Patient*) to share their wisdom with Hollywood hopefuls.

Finally, several organizations run film series throughout the year. Call the following numbers for information about schedules, prices, and memberships: the **Canadian Film Institute** (232-6727), the **Ottawa Film Society** (598-4686), and the international film series at the **University of Ottawa** (562-5800, extension 3748).

SECRET

MURALS

Blink and you'll miss a charming mural portraying the history of francophones in the Ottawa Valley. That's because it's bizarrely hidden away in a little dead-end alley running beside the Giant Tiger store in the Byward Market, at the corner of George and Dalhousie Streets. Easier to see is the huge mural commemorating the **Hull International Bicycle Festival**, which takes up most of the side of a five-storey office building at the corner of Place du Portage and Hôtel de Ville in Hull. Also in Hull, you'll find three exuberant murals created in 1985 to mark the International Year of Youth: *Development* (106 Sacré-Coeur Boulevard), *Participation* (74 Eddy Street), and *Peace* (59 Eddy Street).

SECRET

MUSEUMS

So you think you've seen everything in Ottawa's museums? Have you seen the incongruous flour sifter in the polar bear diorama at the **Canadian Museum of Nature** (240 McLeod Street, 566-4700)? Clarence Tillenius, who designed most of the museum's dioramas in the 1950s and 1960s, was a stickler for detail. He used the sifter to get the artificial snow to drift just right, but a worker carefully backing out of the exhibit (to avoid leaving footprints) left the sifter behind, and the kitchen implement was sealed into the diorama for all eternity. Look in the back left corner.

Meanwhile, once you've checked out the totem poles and other historical tidbits at the **Canadian Museum of Civilization**, don't miss the **Canadian Postal Museum** under the same roof (100 Laurier Street, Hull, Quebec, 819-776-7008), where the history of stamps and philately is presented in a surprisingly entertaining way.

You can live through a simulated earthquake at the **Ecomusée** (170 Montcalm Street, Hull, Quebec, 819-595-7790, www.ecomusee. ville.hull.qc.ca), a natural-science museum that also houses an insectarium with 5,000 creepy specimens, a collection of local minerals, and a replica of an Alberta dinosaur. Interestingly for an ecological museum, it includes exhibits on the industries that arose to take advantage of the Ottawa Valley's natural resources, including logging companies, mines, and Canada's first cement factory. The museum itself is on a splendid site overlooking Brewery Creek, where kids can get in touch with nature by watching the ducks.

I live not far from the **Museum of Classical Antiquities** (Arts Hall, University of Ottawa, 70 Laurier Avenue East, 562-5800, extension 1650), and I'd never heard of it before I started researching this book. Housed in a small, sunny room on the ground floor of a fairly new building, it presents a low-key collection of 2,500 Greek and Roman urns, amphorae, oil lamps, coins, and other small items. The place is run by the university's classics department and focuses on items from between the 7th century BC and the 7th century AD. There are no interactive multimedia panels or any of the other gizmos that dominate most modern museums, just rows of unadorned glass cases. Hours vary, so call ahead. Staffed by student volunteers, it's open regular hours during the school year and in the summer by appointment.

The big national museums do an excellent job of describing Canada's past, but for a good picture of local history head to one of the smaller civic museums. Your options include the **Nepean Museum** (16 Rowley Avenue, Nepean, 723-7936) and the **Gloucester Museum** (4550B Bank Street, Gloucester, 822-2076). The **Cumberland Heritage Village Museum** (2940 Queen Street, Cumberland, 833-3059) is a collection of more than 20 buildings — a blacksmith shop, a schoolhouse, a train station, and others — arranged like a turn-of-the-century Ottawa Valley village.

It's easy to miss the **Bytown Museum** (Entrance Locks, Rideau Canal, 234-4570) tucked away in the Rideau Canal valley between Parliament Hill and the Chateau Laurier. But this is where the city began — the museum is housed in Ottawa's oldest stone building, dating from the 1830s. Inside, the exhibits tell the story of Colonel John By and his dogged team of canal builders as well as other aspects of the city's history.

There's a good chance that you'll be the only person prowling through the **Archives in the Market** (136 St. Patrick Street, 995-5138). The small, two-storey building used to house the sadly missed Canadian Museum of Caricature; when that initiative fizzled, the National Archives of Canada converted the building into a general exhibition space. The last time that I dropped in, there was a great exhibition of art photos of Canadian holidays throughout the 20th century; the pictures of Second World War soldiers celebrating Christmas with local children and of Ukrainian families painting Easter eggs were oddly affecting. But the only other soul there was the security guard, who politely asked me if I'd like her to turn down the radio keeping her company in the echoing space. It's free and often intriguing; drop in if you're shopping in the Byward Market. If nothing else, there are large, clean public restrooms on the second floor.

SECRET
MUSIC

Tired of top 40 and the big chains? **Organized Sound** (354-A Elgin Street, 2nd floor, 233-4900) sells plenty of music that you won't hear on the radio. Ever. It's just the place to go to satisfy that craving for Brazilian experimental jazz or anything else that your mom has never heard of and yet is certain will warp your mind.

Dalhousie Street is another good bet for the latest alternative music. At the north end is **Downtown Records** (201 Dalhousie Street, 241-6466), where you can find urban, house, reggae, and dance tracks of all sorts. At the opposite end of the street, near Besserer Street, **Bowggy Records** (407 Dalhousie Street, 562-1521) claims to be the "home of the alternative movement" and stocks DJ equipment, videos, magazines, CDs, and vinyl.

One of the biggest and best independent record stores in town is the venerable **Record Runner** (212 Rideau Street, 241-3987, www.recordrunner.on.ca), which has such a wide-ranging stock that both the coolest club kids and their boomer parents can probably find something that attracts their attention.

I always thought that the great thing about CDs is that they're impossible to scratch, but apparently they aren't. If yours are skipping and giving you grief, take them to the CD **Repairman** (182 St. Joseph Boulevard, Hull, Quebec, 776-0988) for a little TLC.

Think the world just hasn't been right since Sid Vicious died? Call **Ottawa Punk Rock Listings** (234-PUNX) for the latest concert information.

There are a number of decent used-CD shops in town; most of them also sell videos and tapes. I like **Record Centre** (1097 Wellington

Street, 722-4128) and **The Turning Point** (411 Cooper Street, 230-4586), where the choices range from pop to classical and jazz, and few items cost more than $10.

The latest tunes from Spain, Portugal, Italy, and South America aren't easy to find in the nation's capital. Try the unprepossessing **International Musicland** (St. Laurent Shopping Centre, 1200 St. Laurent Boulevard, 746-3913), where you can dig up discs by artists such as Biagio Antonacci and Rey Ruiz.

SECRET
MUSICAL
INSTRUMENTS

The selection of new and used guitars, amps, keyboards, and brass, woodwind, and percussion instruments at **Song Bird Music** (388 Gladstone Avenue, 594-5323, www.songbirdmusic.com/ottawa/index.html) is so extensive that the store recently expanded to a second location across the street. You'll find everything from 1980s synthesizers for next to nothing to vintage electric guitars that cost as much as a decent used car. The place draws both serious musicians and budget-minded parents.

If you know the difference between a dulcimer and a bowed psaltery — they're both stringed instruments, for those of you out of the loop — you'll be in your element at the **Ottawa Folklore Centre** (1111 Bank Street, 730-2887, www.ottawafolklore.com). You can buy new and used instruments, sign up for a class, and hang out with lots of like-minded musical souls.

SECRET
NEW AGE

A strip of undistinguished storefronts across from a theological university might seem like a strange place for a community of alternative businesses to take root and grow. But that's exactly what has happened on Main Street in Ottawa East, between Hazel and Herridge Streets. At the south end of the row is a health-food shop called **The Wheat Berry** (206 Main Street, 235-7580), where you can buy organic vegetables, butter for vegans, soy milk, tofu, and environmentally friendly toiletries and cleaners, among other products. Next door is **Singing Pebble Books** (202a Main Street, 230-9165), a laid-back place well stocked with books on spirituality, astrology, journal writing, vegetarian cooking, witches, homeopathy, and similar topics. You can also pick up incense, candles, tapes, and dream catchers. My favourite store in the row, however, is **3 Trees** (202 Main Street, 230-0304), a cool little shop that doesn't really fit into any known category. There's stuff from around the world, but it's all much funkier than the inventory of any Pier 1 Imports you'll ever see. There are hemp shirts and tie-dyed dresses, Hindu figurines and Greek Orthodox icons, colourful rugs and throw pillows fit for a harem, CDs, jewellery, fabric purses, and strings of bells. Keep your eye open for the large black-and-white rabbit, which has a habit of conking out in the middle of the hardwood floor. **The Green Door** (see Secret Vegetarian) rounds off the block.

SECRET

NEWSSTANDS

For the combination of selection and knowledgeable staff, no other newsstand in town compares with **Mags and Fags** (254 Elgin Street, 233-9651), which boasts some 6,000 titles in every conceivable category. Every procrastinating, insomniac freelance writer in the greater Ottawa area has probably wandered into this place at one time or another; I'm constantly running into acquaintances here. It's pretty well the best place in town for international newspapers, foreign-language magazines, and periodicals in offbeat categories such as dollmaking and screenwriting.

Maison de la Presse Internationale (92 Bank Street, 230-9774) used to be the closest competitor of Mags and Fags in terms of size and choice. Although it moved to smaller digs a few years ago, it still offers a pretty good selection. Not surprisingly, given that it's part of a worldwide chain with its roots in France, the array of francophone periodicals is excellent.

Globe Mags and Cigars (57 William Street, 241-7274) stocks more than 2,000 titles, but the main drawback is that you have to fight your way to the racks and then fight for your right to root through the magazines stacked up like sardines in a vertical can. The place is tiny, and, since it has a prime location in the busiest part of the Byward Market, it is always packed. Claustrophobic people are happier elsewhere.

Love it or hate it, **Chapters** draws so many customers that it can offer a mind-boggling variety of publications. The flagship store across from the Rideau Centre (47 Rideau Street, 241-0073) has the most diverse selection of the chain's five Ottawa locations. One of the best things about browsing at Chapters is that, unlike other newsstands that post signs such as "This is not a library" and "Don't read it, buy it," Chapters boldly encourages you to browse. Granted, the store recently removed the benches once conveniently located next to the magazine racks. But they weren't that comfortable anyway. Take your selections and find one of the cozy chairs scattered throughout the store (the ones on the second floor are less likely to be occupied).

In the near west end, **Wellington Street News** (1308 Wellington Street, 798-0331) has a good selection of magazines in all categories, including some German and Italian publications. The jazz music often wafting overhead is a nice bonus.

Britton's Smoke Shop (844 Bank Street, 235-6826) is particularly strong in news magazines — not surprisingly, since its location in the Glebe makes it a magnet for neighbourhood politicos and journalists.

Finally, the **Daily News Smokery** (Gloucester Centre, 1980 Ogilvie Road, 748-6397) has a good selection of British, French, and German magazines as well as the usual North American titles.

S E C R E T
NONSMOKING

I'm not a nonsmoking fanatic, but I do like to eat dinner without clouds of nicotine wafting across my plate. And, even though provincial laws require almost all restaurants to provide nonsmoking sections, sometimes they just don't do the job. It's not much good sitting in a "nonsmoking" section if the folks at a table four feet away in the smoking section are happily puffing away. A number of restaurants are completely nonsmoking, either because they want to attract smoke-averse patrons or because they're too small to properly ventilate separate areas. Try **Trattoria Zingaro** (Italian, 10-18 Beechwood Avenue, 744-6509), **New Delhi** (683 Bank Street, 237-4041), the **National Arts Centre Café** (Canadian, 53 Elgin Street, 594-5127), or **Lapointe's Seafood Grill** (55 York Street, 241-6221). The Regional Municipality of Ottawa-Carleton has also compiled a list of non-smoking restaurants (www.rmoc.on.ca/pictures/smokefree-ottawa.html).

SECRET
OASES

When it's minus 40 with the windchill and it feels like years since you've been warm, head for one of Ottawa's indoor gardens. The **Bank of Canada** (234 Wellington Street, garden entrance on Sparks Street) has one that features a pretty pond, palm trees, and prayer plants, and you can see bureaucrats at work in the offices lining the atrium. But the best thing is the oddball Yap stone in the middle of the pond, a three-ton piece of limestone once used as currency on the island of Yap in the South Pacific. A few blocks away, the **Clarica building** (99 Bank Street) has a larger atrium with the bonus of a few places to buy and eat lunch.

After a blustery winter day exploring the Byward Market, you'll enjoy the two sky-lit courtyards inside the **National Gallery of Canada** (380 Sussex Drive, 990-1985). My favourite is the rather austere marble water court, where you can look through a glass-bottomed pool at people wandering the floor below.

The eternal emptiness of the red-brick atrium at **Fifth Avenue Court** (Bank Street between Fourth and Fifth Avenues) is a continuing mystery to me. There's everything a solace seeker might need: a fountain, a bakery, a coffeeshop, and natural light. However, aside from the nannies who sometimes drop in with their young charges in the mornings, it's largely deserted. It's a great place to take a break during a chilly Christmas-shopping expedition in the Glebe's nifty gift shops.

SECRET
PARKING

First a word of warning: the green hornets (Ottawa's parking police) take their job seriously, and Ottawa's complicated parking laws give them many opportunities to make their quotas. If you're parking on a street downtown, read the signs carefully. Generally, you can't park on many major arteries in the core during either morning or evening rush hour, and the green hornets won't think twice about towing your vehicle. If your car is missing, call 244-5444 to see where it ended up.

Given these drawbacks, off-street parking may make more sense. Unfortunately, some lots charge you roughly the equivalent of the gross national product of Bolivia for the privilege of leaving your car in their not-so-tender care for a few hours.

So what do you do? Fortunately, there are a few downtown lots with decent prices, many of them run by the city (Ottawans' tax dollars at

work). Try the city-owned garage at 141 Clarence Street, just east of Dalhousie in the Byward Market, or the city lot and garage at 190 Slater Street, between Bank and O'Connor.

If you don't mind a short walk and a sometimes frustrating search for a space, you can park for free on some residential streets between Elgin Street and the Rideau Canal and on various streets south of Gloucester Street.

Finally, the enormous parking lot between the National Library of Canada and the Supreme Court of Canada is cluttered with signs saying "Permit holders only." And, during the week, they mean it. But on weekends the place is largely deserted. Parking there is a calculated risk, so don't blame me if you get a ticket. However, if you don't mind a little uphill hike, it offers great access to Parliament Hill.

SECRET
PARLIAMENT HILL

Most of the Centre Block went up in a blaze one night in February 1916, but firefighters managed to save the original **cornerstone** as well as the Parliamentary Library. The cornerstone was relaid by the Duke of Connaught later that year on the northeast corner of the building.

Every year, the interior of the **Centre Block** is decorated to the hilt for Christmas (or, as the ever politically correct bureaucrats insist on calling it, "the holiday season"). Whatever it's called, it's a good excuse to haul an enormous conifer into the main rotunda and drape it with lights and to deck the official halls with boughs of just about everything available. The Centre Block usually holds an open house from 4:30 p.m. to 8:30 p.m. each evening from a few days before Christmas until the day after New Year's. If you're in town, don't miss it; with its gothic arches swathed in greenery and bows, the place really is magical. In particular, try to get there right at 4:30, just as the winter sun disappears; the window at the end of the west rotunda corridor gives off an unearthly glow then, setting the whole limestone hallway on fire (metaphorically, of course).

If you want to see for yourself what the "action" during **Question Period** in the House of Commons is like, call your MP and reserve passes to the public galleries. (You can also ask for passes at the visitor centre (992-4793) on a first-come, first-served basis, but Question Period is popular, and sometimes there's little room available.) QP, as hill staffers call it, usually starts at 2 p.m. Mondays through Thursdays and at 11 a.m. on Fridays when the House is in session. When I first saw it, I was astonished by how few people were actually there; those clips you see on the evening news are the products of TV-savvy politicians. They scurry to sit behind the MP most likely to score the day's sound bite and then move back to their scattered seats when the moment of high drama passes and the discussion moves back to mundane topics such as National Hatband Week. One little-known fact: the galleries in the House (but not the Senate) are equipped with listening devices for people with hearing aids. Both galleries have earphones that provide instant translations of statements in either English or French. Avoid the galleries like the plague in June, when they're packed with rowdy 12 year olds visiting the capital on end-of-school-year trips.

Just about everyone who visits Parliament Hill signs up for the Centre Block tour, which is well worth doing. But fewer people know that

they can also tour a few rooms in the **East Block** that have been restored to their appearance at the time of Confederation. Call 239-5000 for information.

Of course, you should sign up for the Centre Block tour too. It's one of the highlights of any trip to the capital. For that reason, the crowds of people waiting to take the tour on any given summer day can be daunting. Want an easy way to beat the lineups? Head to the National Capital Commission's Info-Tent (where tours are organized) during the Changing the Guard ceremony at 10 a.m. As everyone tries to get a good look at the ceremony, you can probably nab a few tickets with little or no wait.

SECRET
PASTA

The great thing about **Parma Ravioli** (1314 Wellington Street, 722-4011) is its simplicity. One big board lists about a dozen kinds of handmade pasta, with their prices by weight. Another board lists nine kinds of fresh sauces. Aside from some Italian soft drinks, a few prepackaged meals such as lasagna, and some accoutrements such as olive oil and balsamic vinegar, that's all the store sells. It has settled on one product, which it makes very well.

If you'd rather eat someone else's pasta than cook it yourself, here's my favourite neighbourhood secret: a tiny 30-seat restaurant called the **Eclectic Noodle** (287-B Somerset Street East, 234-2428), hidden away on a residential street in Sandy Hill. The chef there has a marvellous way with pasta, and the daily special is almost always worth investigating. Reservations are essential.

S E C R E T

PHOTOGRAPHY

Most visitors to Ottawa can't leave without snapping a few shots of the Peace Tower, the city's most recognizable symbol. However, instead of standing on the main lawn to take your photos, like everyone else does, try these suggestions.

If you want to get your family in the picture, line them up on the staircase on the east side of the **West Block** (be careful not to get in the way of busy hill staffers and MPs hurrying in and out of the building). This location gives you a great perspective on the Peace Tower and its flag.

To capture the hill from the east side, stroll along the terrace between the **Chateau Laurier** (1 Rideau Street) and the **Rideau Canal**. Follow it to **Major's Hill Park**, where you can capture great tulip beds in the foreground each spring.

The **National Gallery of Canada** (380 Sussex Drive, 990-1985) provides several unique views of the back of Parliament Hill. Shoot through the glass pyramid of the enormous Great Hall, or take an unobstructed view from the terrace of the cafeteria. Or you can get an excellent shot of the hill cradled between the two undulating wings of the **Canadian Museum of Civilization** (100 Laurier Street, Hull, Quebec, 819-776-7000) from the sidewalk near that museum's main entrance. To have greenery rather than buildings framing your shot, follow the bicycle path that cuts across the back lawn of the museum; going east will bring you to **Jacques Cartier Park**, but going west will give you a more unobstructed shot.

From the other side of the hill, you can get a shot that includes the National Gallery of Canada and Notre-Dame Cathedral Basilica, as well as Parliament Hill, from the parking lot behind the **Supreme Court of Canada** (Wellington Street, 995-4330).

Strangely, one of the most photogenic views of the Peace Tower can be found at the **Beechwood Cemetery** (280 Beechwood Avenue, 741-9530). The pretty gazebo in the Botanical Cremation Gardens forms a perfect frame for the Peace Tower, several miles away.

For twilight-loving shutterbugs, the **Laurier Bridge** over the Rideau Canal is a perfect place to capture the sunset behind the Peace Tower. Set up your tripod on the small platform at the top of the stairs leading to the canal and you won't obstruct foot traffic.

Got enough shots of Parliament Hill? Then check out some of Ottawa's other scenic sites. I like **Rockcliffe Park** (Rockcliffe Parkway), probably for sentimental reasons: we had our wedding photos taken at the stone bandshell there. You can also spot blushing brides on any summer Saturday in the **Arboretum** at the Central Experimental Farm.

In the spring, you can get great shots of the Canadian Museum of Civilization, framed by lilacs, from the lookout behind the **West Block** on Parliament Hill. And in the Glebe, the bridge spanning **Patterson Creek** at O'Connor Street is a scenic bit of Victoriana.

Shutterbugs who want to buy professional-quality film or a new or used camera head to **Ginn Photographic** (433 Bank Street, 567-4686) or the **Focus Centre** (254 Bank Street, 232-5368, or 501 Hazeldean Road, Kanata, 836-1016).

Finally, to see often unsettling but usually intriguing works by modern photographers, don't miss the **Canadian Museum of Contemporary Photography** (1 Rideau Canal, next to the Chateau Laurier, 990-8257, www.cmcp.gallery.ca). Admission is free, and there's a tiny but fun gift shop.

SECRET
PIANO BARS

For a gentlemen's club sort of ambience, head to **Friday's Roast Beef House** (150 Elgin Street, 237-5353), where more likely than not the pianist in the wood-panelled bar upstairs will know *Misty*. A few blocks away, at the **Full House** (337 Somerset Street West, 238-6734), you'll feel like you're in a London bomb shelter during the blitz as old-fashioned standards such as *Roll Out the Barrel* and *Knees Up Mother Brown* get everyone singing. At **Zoé's** in the Chateau Laurier (1 Rideau Street, 241-1414), the mood amid the potted palms and marble columns is subdued and elegant.

SECRET
PICNICS

Make your picnic an event by having it "catered." Several local caterers do gourmet takeout that lends itself well to a special picnic. The menus at these places change frequently, so call ahead to see what's available. Many will take special orders for just about any dish that you desire if you phone a few days in advance. Try **Thyme and Again** (1320 Wellington Street, 722-0093), **Blackbird Catering** (1200 Bank Street, 730-0774, www.blackbirdcatering.com), **Hopewell Kitchen** (70-A Leonard Avenue, 730-6363), or **Epicuria** (419 MacKay Street, 745-7356, www.epicuria.ca).

Once the food is arranged, it's time to pick a picnic spot. In a city with so many parks and wild areas, you're bound to get lots of debate on the perfect place. My favourites include the **Black Rapids lockstation** on the Rideau Canal, **Vincent Massey Park** (the north side, near Carleton University and far from the large groups that often take over the south end of the park), and just about anywhere in **Gatineau Park**.

SECRET
PIZZA

Ask anyone who's lived near downtown Ottawa in the past couple of decades who makes the best pizza, and I can guarantee you that almost everyone will say **Café Colonnade** (280 Metcalfe Street, 237-3179). What makes it so incredibly good? I think it's the sauce, but others say it's the crust, and many mention the incredible cheesiness. This is a thick, fresh, calorie-packed pie for serious pizza connoisseurs. It's eat in or take out only at the downtown location, but a second east-end outlet (1754 Montreal Road, 745-0000) delivers.

Fans of **Pavarazzi's** (491 Somerset Street West, 233-2320, and 223 Laurier Avenue East, 233-3222) square gourmet pizzas are legion.

While many sit-down restaurants will serve up concoctions involving exotic ingredients, this is one of the few delivery places that will bring you a pie topped with smoked salmon, capers and red onions, or chicken, garlic, and sun-dried tomato pesto. You can also get salads, panzerotti, exotic pastas (seafood fettuccine with basil pesto, anyone?), and Italian soft drinks such as Brio Chinotto and Limonata.

When I was at Carleton University, we practically lived on takeout pizza. **Calabria** (193 Bell Street North, 235-4711) is a perennial favourite with Carleton students, while the tangy pizzas at **Fida's** (44 Seneca Street, 730-6800) are so gooey that we used to call them slop-zas.

Strangely, I haven't found an all-night pizza joint in Ottawa. The closest thing is probably **Season's Pizza** (288 Booth Street, 237-8080), which is open until 5 a.m. on Fridays and Saturdays and 4 a.m. the rest of the week; it delivers to all the downtown hotels.

SECRET
POETRY

In a small heritage row house in the Byward Market, poet John Bart Gerald and his partner, artist Julie Maas, run a unique art gallery/poetry shop called, naturally enough, **Gerald & Maas** (202 St. Patrick Street, 241-1312, www.achilles.net/~jbgerald). Most of the items on sale were created by Gerald, Maas, or other members of their creative family (Gerald's mother's paintings, for example, hang in New York's Whitney Museum). The exquisitely printed small volumes of Gerald's poetry, illustrated with Maas's etchings, are artworks in their

own right. It's worth dropping in just to pass the time with Gerald, whose newcomer's takes on Ottawa (he and Maas moved here from Maine in the mid-1990s to be closer to a daughter in Montreal) are dead-on and funny. Proof of the friendly, casual nature of the whole enterprise is on the sign on the door: "Usually open."

SECRET
POLITICIANS

Spotting politicians outside their native lair isn't always easy. For one thing, backbenchers aren't the most famous faces in Canada, unless you're one of those rare people whose TV is frequently switched to CPAC. But the probabilities rise the closer you are to Parliament Hill. The **Chateau Laurier** (1 Rideau Street, 241-1414) and its restaurants and lounge are good places to spot politicos, particularly when major meetings are taking place in the **Government Conference Centre** across the street. A tunnel running beneath Rideau Street connects the two buildings, giving politicians a quick escape from whichever protesters are picketing their meetings that week. **Mamma Teresa's** (300 Somerset Street West, 236-3023) has long been a favourite with politicians, who come to relax over huge plates of veal parmigiana or fettuccine alfredo. **Hy's Steakhouse** (170 Queen Street, 234-4545) is popular with the meat-and-potatoes political crowd.

You have to be a member or a member's guest, or be attending a special public event, to get into the **National Press Club** (150 Wellington Street, 233-5641, www.pressclub.on.ca), right across the road from Parliament Hill. But if you hang around the Wellington Street door, you may see the PM, a cabinet minister, or other bigwig darting inside on the way to a news conference (many of which are filmed in a small, blue-curtained studio in the bowels of the building).

Even big politicos have to buy their smokes and toothpaste some-where. Many drop in to the **Green Dragon** (179 Sparks Street, 233-5455), a Chinese convenience store steps from Parliament Hill that stocks a little of just about everything. Even if you don't spot a famous face, you might pick up a bit of insider gossip.

The situation for political groupies may improve soon. The internal restaurants on Parliament Hill have been bleeding money for years. And, even though the once notoriously subsidized prices have been quietly raised, the flow of red ink shows little sign of slowing down. As this book was being written, there was talk of opening the restau-rants on the hill itself to the great unwashed masses. Traditionally, the various cafeterias and the crown jewel — the fancy **Parliamen-tary Restaurant** on the sixth floor of the Centre Block — have been open only to MPs, senators, hill staffers, members of the Press Gallery, and their guests. When my husband worked as an aide to an MP in the early 1990s, his boss once invited us to lunch at the hallowed precincts of the Parliamentary Restaurant (usually off limits to mere staff). If the place is opened to the public by the time that this book is published, your best chances of spotting famous faces will be on Wednesdays, when many MPs are in the building to attend caucus meetings. Call the main information number for the House of Commons (992-4793) to find out whether you should start pressing your Sunday suit.

SECRET
PORTUGUESE

There's nothing fancy about **Casa Do Churrasco** (190 Dalhousie Street, 241-2743), which serves up Portuguese barbecue in a converted Kentucky Fried Chicken outlet. There's a TV playing European rock videos, some posters of Lisbon, a set of wall tiles portraying a pretty Old World cottage, and about 10 tables draped with red-and-white-checked plastic tablecloths. But you're not here for the ambience: you're here for loaded plates of cheap barbecued pork, chicken, and ribs, along with heaps of sizzling fries. The service is fast and friendly, and the place offers takeout.

SECRET
PRESCRIPTIONS

No, it's not what you think. The **Glebe Apothecary** (778 Bank Street, 234-8587) makes prescriptions for those who agree with Mary Poppins that a spoonful of something other than chemicals makes the medicine go down. You can choose from more than 20 flavourings to camouflage your toddler's antibiotics or your own cough medicine.

S E C R E T
PRINTS

Pack Rabbit (322 Richmond Road, 761-1601) is best known as a place for Asian goods, such as origami paper, chopsticks, sashimi dishes, feng shui manuals, and roasted seaweed. But at the back of the store, you'll find one of Ottawa's most eclectic selections of art posters and prints. Scores of shops in town will sell you a giant photograph of Elvis, Marilyn, or Bogie. But there aren't many places where you can find pinups of Coco Chanel and Robert Burns. There are plenty of great black-and-white art photos and a fun selection of offbeat postcards (many of which themselves would look good framed).

If you're looking for British hunting prints, 19th-century architectural drawings, or vintage fashion plates to decorate your study, try **The Astrolabe Gallery** (71 Sparks Street, 234-2348) or **G. Dreeke** (inside Bank Street Antiques, 1136 Bank Street, 730-0084). Both shops specialize in antique prints, most of them over 100 years old.

S E C R E T
PUBLIC ART

Like any capital city, Ottawa is peppered with statues of dead politicians, monuments to various national events, and artworks given to the city by foreign governments for all kinds of reasons. Then there are the bits and pieces of public art placed around town for our collective edification. Most of the attention goes to the biggies, such as the **National War Memorial** on Confederation Square (which never fails to affect me no matter how often I see it) and the official sculptures of prime ministers that dot Parliament Hill. Here's the best of the rest.

Two whimsical downtown sculptures are guaranteed people pleasers. On a small lawn bordered by the National Arts Centre, the Rideau Canal, and the Rideau Street bridge, the cheerful sculpture called *Balancing* is usually covered with kids imitating the cartoonish people staking out their places on a long beam. I like the grumpy bureaucrat, with his horn rims and proper suit, glaring at the insufficiently serious folk at the other end of the beam. Created by New Brunswick artist John Hooper in 1981, it is designed to represent the various people who call Ottawa home. Its style reminds me a bit of *McClintock's Dream* (inside the Byward Market Building, York and William Streets), a fanciful papier-mâché piece created three years earlier by Victor Tolgesy. A sinuous cloud filled with people, it's suspended from the rafters above the market's food stalls. The same artist also did the strangely captivating *Explorer II* (on the grounds of the Théâtre de l'Île, Hull), a 1968 abstract piece inspired by the final preparations for the 1969 moon landing.

I also like the charming *Secret Bench of Knowledge* (near the National Library of Canada, 395 Wellington Street) as much for itself as for its history. It just appeared one morning in the early 1990s, dropped off in the night by artist Lea Vivot. There was great consternation among public officials at this random act of artwork. There had been no competition, no juries, no official stamp of approval. It wasn't in the plan. The consensus among the bigwigs seemed to be that people couldn't just go about donating sculptures and leaving them anywhere they pleased. So Vivot took it away, but the public — unlike the powers that be — had grown fond of the sculpture of a young man holding an apple while nuzzling his girlfriend. Eventually, a copy of the work was donated to the city and placed in the same spot. Look for the engraved messages on the sculpture celebrating reading.

Thankfully, the sculpture of *Terry Fox* (Wellington Street at Metcalfe Street) is no longer such a secret, since it has finally been moved to a prominent place right across from Parliament Hill. In 1983, sculptor John Hooper immortalized Fox, the young man with cancer whose 1981 fund-raising run ended tragically when the disease attacked his lungs. To our national shame, however, the statue was stuck for years in a dingy underpass beneath Colonel By Drive near the Rideau Centre.

Only in Ottawa could we misplace two enormous sculptures for half a century. In 1912, sculptor Walter Allward began work on the figures of justice and truth (*Justicia* and *Veritas*) that now regally flank the front doors of the **Supreme Court of Canada** (Wellington Street at Kent Street). Then Allward was distracted by the opportunity to build the Canadian war memorial at Vimy Ridge. Somehow (no one seems to be taking the blame), his plaster forms ended up in cartons in a government parking lot, where they came to light in 1969. The following year, they were cast in bronze and installed in their current home.

The **Regional Municipality of Ottawa-Carleton**'s headquarters (111 Lisgar Street, 560-1335) is home to some of Ottawa's most intriguing public art. On the northwest side of the plaza that fronts onto Laurier Avenue near the Rideau Canal is a group of abstract works. Artist Michael Bussières titled this piece *Virtual Instrument Paradigm*, but almost everyone else calls it "that talking sculpture." When people walk by, the piece emits odd noises that sound like leftover sound effects from *Plan Nine from Outer Space*. Meanwhile, the oldest section of the headquarters — a Victorian limestone pile that was once the Ottawa Normal School — has all kinds of heads and symbols carved into it. On the south façade are a child's face and an owl, evoking the building's roots as a teachers' college, while various bearded dudes look down from the main façade on Elgin Street.

At the south end of Dalhousie Street, in front of Les Suites Hotel, you'll find a lonely statue of **Simon Bolivar**, donated to the city in the late 1980s. A huge debate ensued about where to put this unsolicited memorial; it was eventually relegated to this out-of-the-way intersection.

Also a little off the beaten path is a touching memorial to the Vietnamese who risked everything to escape to Canada and other countries in the late 1970s and early 1980s. **Refugee Mother and Child** (Somerset Street West at Preston Street), by Toronto artist Pham The Trung, stands in the heart of Ottawa's Vietnamese Canadian community.

On the Transitway, Ottawa's buses-only system of roads, keep your eyes open for the often whimsical pieces by local artists that the regional government has installed in sometimes unexpected places. There's **mem-o-mobilia** near the Billings Bridge station by artist Mark Marsters, a playful reflection on turn-of-the-century advertising billboards. The same artist did **Salute/Salut**, a series of four hands that wave, point, or give you signals along the rock-cut section of the Transitway near the Ottawa River Parkway. At the Pleasant Park station, artist Susan Feindel has used vivid pieces of stained glass to evoke a plowed hillside on an otherwise featureless concrete wall.

S E C R E T
PUBS

OK, **Patty's Pub** (1186 Bank Street, 730-2434) isn't much of a secret. In its present location, and its previous incarnation about half a mile farther up Bank Street, it's been slaking the thirsts of Ottawans in this neighbourhood for a couple of decades. Usually, patrons head right for the fireplace room at the back, which is undeniably charming. But many don't even know that there's a private little parlour at the front of the pub, just big enough for one table and maybe eight chairs, with wide windows overlooking Bank Street. It's the perfect place for a raucous group of friends to get together for a loud laugh with no fear of disturbing nearby quiet types.

On a cold winter night, there are fewer cozier pubs in the capital than **Alfie's** (14 Waller Street, 241-5050), snuggled into the lower floor of a 19th-century marble factory. It's not as insanely busy as the watering holes in the nearby Byward Market, and it really does feel like a neighbourhood local from the old country.

Homesick easterners can often be found amid the patrons at the **Newfoundland Pub** (940 Montreal Road, 745-0962), where you can tuck into cod cheeks while listening to Celtic tunes. If cod cheeks aren't your thing, you can always play a round of darts.

The **Pickwick Pub** (422 MacKay Street, 742-3169) is an anomaly: an authentic-feeling pub that also serves tasty, trendy food. The prices are a little steeper than at your average beer joint, but the food is much better. The weekend breakfast items, in particular, are small works of art, garnished with fresh fruit and other things that you don't usually associate with beer halls. Another pub that gets high marks for its breakfasts is the **Manx Pub** (370 Elgin Street, 231-2070).

Sometimes you have to drive a bit to find a secret, and the **Cheshire Cat Pub** (2193 Richardson Sideroad, Carp, 831-2183) on the western fringes of the capital is no exception. However, if you like Celtic music and loads of atmosphere, it's worth the drive to this little pub hidden in a former church. It's popular with mountain bikers looking for an ice-cold brew after plowing through the mud along the nearby Kanata Lakes trails. Call ahead to find out when the next jam session is scheduled.

SECRET

ROMANCE

Romance . . . in Ottawa? I can just hear the snickers: what does a city populated by number-crunching bureaucrats and high-tech chip-heads know about *l'amour*? Well, with a winter that lasts for six months some years, we've had to come up with all kinds of ways to amuse ourselves and stay warm at the same time.

One of the best spots in Ottawa for nocturnal nuzzling is **Tin House Court**, a charming square hidden between Clarence and Murray Streets just east of Sussex Drive. The place gets its name from the elaborate two-storey façade that now hangs, somewhat incongruously, high on a wall on the northwest inside corner of the square. A 19th-century tinsmith named Honoré Foisy built it for his own home, which once stood nearby. When the building was torn down in 1961, preservationists managed to save a bit of the fanciful façade; the rest was rebuilt by local artist Art Price in 1973. The square below has a small fountain surrounded by park benches, trees, wooden planters spilling over with flowers, and café patios. On summer nights, when the fountain and the spire of Notre-Dame Cathedral Basilica a block away are both softly lit, the square truly is magical.

I have a soft spot for the nearby **Alexandra Bridge** (connecting St. Patrick Street in Ottawa to Laurier Street in Hull), especially at Christmastime. In December and early January, parks and streets on both sides of the Ottawa River are illuminated with thousands of multicoloured lights strung through the trees. The best view of the lights is from this bridge, where you can see a panorama that takes in the Canadian Museum of Civilization and Parliament Hill. When my husband and I were dating, I happened to mention to him how much I loved this view. One December evening, he collected me in a limousine, popped open a bottle of champagne, and proposed to me at midnight in the middle of the Alexandra Bridge. It may not be romantic to everyone, but it worked for us.

If snuggling on a park bench is your idea of romance, then the benches overlooking the Ottawa River in **Andrew Haydon Park** are a perfect place to watch the sun set over the Gatineau Hills in a blaze of glory. At the same time of the evening, the benches along the east side of the **Rideau Canal** between the Rideau Centre and the University of Ottawa give you an excellent view of the sunset behind the Peace Tower. Early morning is a wonderful time to linger on a bench beside the Rideau River in **Strathcona Park**; if it's quiet, you may spot a blue heron.

Brighton House Bed and Breakfast (306-308 First Avenue, 233-7777) has a lovely suite with a big brass bed. Perhaps because you can enjoy a champagne breakfast on the suite's balcony, the inn earned a high rating of three and a half lips (I'm not making this up) on the TV series *Best Places to Kiss*. And at the **Carmichael Inn and**

Spa (46 Cartier Street, 236-4667, www.carmichaelinn.com), you can book an overnight package for couples that includes a room in the rambling, turn-of-the-century mansion, two massages, and candles for your hydrotherapy bath, as well as breakfast.

At one of the monthly meetings of the **Ottawa Romance Writers Association**, you'll learn what passionate hearts beat under the surface of the bureaucratic capital. There are several published romance writers in the Ottawa area, including yours truly. Since ORWA is a volunteer association, contact numbers and meeting locations are subject to change. Contact the association's parent organization, the Romance Writers of America (281-440-6885, www.rwanational.com), for the most current information.

SECRET
ROOF TERRACES

Unlike many cities, Ottawa is short on downtown greenery; there's no Central Park or Boston Common where asphalt-weary urbanites can enjoy a break. Perhaps because Gatineau Park, a 35,600-hectare area of actual wilderness, is a 15-minute drive from Parliament Hill, no one felt a need to provide much shrubbery, aside from Confederation Park and Major's Hill Park. But don't despair — just look up. Way up. Ottawa's rooftops are alive with plants, vines, and flowering trees.

One of the biggest, most scenic, and least used is the terrace shared by the **Rideau Centre** and the **Ottawa Congress Centre**. Particularly pretty in the spring, when the flowering crabapples put on a pink-and-white show, it's a great place to eat your bag lunch at one of several picnic tables on postage-stamp squares of grass. The west side gives you a nice view of the Rideau Canal and glimpses of the Peace Tower. The only times when it's really busy are in the evenings before or after a movie in the Rideau Centre cinemas. The main entrance from the Rideau Centre is next to the cinemas on the top floor. There are several entrances inside the Congress Centre, or simply take the stairs next to the fountain at the corner of Colonel By Drive and Daly Street.

Another terrace that's largely deserted except in the early evenings is the shady, multilevel one on top of the **National Arts Centre** (53 Elgin Street). Just about opposite the Rideau Centre terrace, it offers a better view of Parliament Hill. To reach it, take the stairs from the Mackenzie King Bridge over the canal or any of the several sets of stairs leading roofward from the main entrance.

SECRET
SANDWICHES

There have been many pretenders: upstart upscale delis, interloping restaurants from Montreal, chain restaurants trying to add a little local colour. But you won't get a better smoked meat sandwich in Ottawa than at **Nate's Deli** (316 Rideau Street, 789-9191). The sandwich is just the way it should be: minimum bread, maximum meat, and lots of artery-hardening potential. And the deli looks like little has changed there since Diefenbaker held sway in the House of Commons up the road; Nate's is still a palace of Formica and chrome. Restaurant owner Dave Smith is something of a local legend; at almost any local charity event, he'll probably be there, cooking up a storm for the good cause.

The sandwiches at the **Budapest Deli** (54 Byward Market, 241-5400) are so enormous that, when I worked in the neighbourhood, I used to buy one and bring half of it back to the office to store in the fridge for the next day. Probably because it offers such great value, the Budapest attracts long lunch-hour lineups.

For a bargain lunch, try **Goldstein's Food Market** (255 Elgin Street, 235-7157), where you can get soup or a salad *and* a sandwich for the princely sum of $1.99.

SECRET
SCOTCH

The **Dunvegan Pub** in Sandy Hill (244 Laurier Avenue East, 569-1301) is the place to go for a dim, smoky, authentic atmosphere in which to quaff your single-malt Scotch. To look at it, you'd think that the place had been here forever, but it just opened in the mid-1990s in a building that was once a drugstore. During the school year, it's often packed with students from the nearby University of Ottawa.

The Barley Mow (1060 Bank Street, 730-1279, and 700 March Road, Kanata, 599-6098, www.barleymow.com) has 32 different single-malt scotches on its menu, including a 25-year-old brew called Highland Park. If you can't make up your mind, try the scotch sampler: six tipples from different distilleries, brought to your table in a little tray of shot glasses. The food here, which takes its inspiration from the diverse countries of the Commonwealth as well as Britain, is better than most pub grub — the curried chicken, in particular, is superb.

The Black Tomato (11 George Street, 789-8123) has a great location in an old stone Byward Market building with deep windowsills and a relatively pleasant cobbled courtyard (sit with your back to the nearby parking lot, and pretend you're in Old Montreal). But the real attractions are the booze, the food, and the tunes. There are 30 single-malt scotches, along with a wide selection of microbrewed drafts and wines by the bottle or glass. The food — listed on what must be the city's heaviest menus, which appear to be attached to pieces of slate — ranges from Thai and Cajun to Greek and Indian, and it comes to your table sizzling hot. And you can while away the time before your meal arrives by browsing through the racks of alternative CDs for sale near the door.

SECRET
SHORTCUT

In an area of Sandy Hill where cross-streets between Laurier Avenue East and the streets to the north are few, some smart soul has built a shady pedestrian shortcut. The path runs between an apartment tower and the High Commission of Brunei and incidentally gives you a good way to observe the outdoor doings of the sultan's minions. Look for the entrance to the path near the intersection of Goulbourn Avenue and Laurier, on the opposite (north) side of the street.

SECRET
SKATING

If you'd love to skate on the Rideau Canal, but you haven't strapped on a pair of blades since you were a kid, you may find the weekend crowds on the ice intimidating. Here's my tip: tackle the canal first thing in the morning. Especially on a weekday, the ice will be largely deserted except for some keen guys in suits skating to work, briefcases dangling from their hands. And the maintenance crews usually do their work at night, so the ice is generally smooth and clean in the morning. Night skating is also good, though I wouldn't do it alone since, if you hurt yourself, few passersby will be around to help. And, of course, every few years some nut comes out to harass women skating alone on the canal at night.

If the busy weekend hours are the most convenient time for you, however, there's still one way to beat the crowds. Head for the two least-busy parts of the canal: the little inlet near First Avenue called Patterson Creek and the stretch between Dows Lake and the Hartwell Locks near Carleton University. Because many skaters don't even realize that they exist, they're often quiet. The only drag is that the maintenance crews sometimes don't maintain them as often as the main stretch of the canal.

SECRET
SKIING

Two hundred miles of groomed cross-country trails and a series of accommodations ranging from simple yurts to full-scale hostels mean that skiers can make their winter way across **Gatineau Park** (819-827-2020) on their own two feet for days at a time. The shelters are often rudimentary, with bunk beds and no drinking water. But they're immensely popular, so reserve them well in advance. One of them, Brown Cabin, is also open to hikers and mountain bikers in the summer and fall.

SECRET
SPA

It's a little off the beaten path, but a short drive past the edge of east-end Orleans takes you to a spa hidden away in an 1835 log house. The **Little House Spa** (2030 Becketts Creek Road, Cumberland, 282-4327, www.littlehousespa.com) offers massages, facials, aromatherapy, and other standard spa treatments. But the setting itself is part of the allure: when you're all relaxed and drowsy after your pampering, you can stroll through the herb garden and more than 80 acres of tamed wilderness.

SECRET
SPANISH

The tapas at **Café Paradiso** (199 Bank Street, 565-0657) are sort of a Latin fusion experience. The chef has ranged far afield for inspiration, so you can nosh on lemongrass chicken satay or Brie marinated in olive oil and fresh herbs, as well as more traditional dishes such as calamari, for between two dollars and five dollars a serving. The funky chairs and sculptural light fixtures add to the international ambience.

Olé Tapas Bar (352 Somerset Street West, 220-9154) is a tiny, 30-seat restaurant/bar where tapas and live Latin music are on the menu seven nights a week. The owner and many of the waiters are musicians too. Friends of the Spanish Language meet here every Monday night for conversational practice.

SECRET
SPORTSWEAR

Pick up exercise shorts, bathing suits, fleeces, and sweatpants at about half the price you'd pay at the yuppie chain stores at **Forbie Activewear** (314 Richmond Road, 724-6167). Funky fabrics are a bonus. Everything's made on site; look behind the counter, and you'll see the seamstresses at work. And, if you don't find what you're looking for, ask about custom orders.

SECRET
SRI LANKAN

Tucked into a tiny space on the ground floor of a nondescript apartment building near the Somerset Theatre is **Ceylonta** (403 Somerset Street West, 237-7812, www.ceylonta.com). Many dishes here will be somewhat familiar to anyone who likes South Indian cuisine, though treats such as string hoppers (strips of meat, noodles, and vegetables) are uniquely Sri Lankan. And, unlike Indian chefs, Sri Lankans quickly roast their spices before grinding them, so flavourings such as tamarind, black mustard, fenugreek, and cardamom have a unique taste. It's a good place for vegetarians looking for something a little different, though there are lots of meat-based dishes too. And, if you'd like to eat in the traditional Sri Lankan way — with your right hand, sans cutlery — the staff will be happy to give you a few tips so that you don't end up with curry on your shirt.

SECRET
SUNDIALS

Some of us just feel as though we give all our money to the government. Max Florence actually did so in 1975, and the sundial in **Rideau Falls Park** by local artist Art Price commemorates his generous gift. And, just down Sussex Drive, you'll find Ottawa's oldest public timepiece: the sundial on the southwest corner of the **Grey Nuns' Mother House** (9 Bruyère Street), installed in 1851.

I'd passed by the large, reddish, abstract sculpture on Sparks Street near O'Connor dozens of times before I learned that it, too, is a sundial. Known as the ***Kinetic Clock***, it serves as a sundial once each year, when the noon-hour sun on June 21 causes it to cast a perfectly rectangular shadow. The four triangles at the top also work as a complicated clock by rotating at different frequencies; at the top of each hour, they line up. I think that I'd rather just check my watch.

S E C R E T
SWANS

No, your eyes aren't deceiving you: if you think that you've spotted an elegant swan amid the flocks of more prosaic ducks and geese on the Rideau River, you probably have. The river is home to the Royal Swans, descendants of 12 swans that Queen Elizabeth II gave to Ottawa in 1967 during Canada's centennial celebrations. There are now about 30 swans; most of them are white mute swans, but there are a few Australian black swans as well. In 1995, there was great consternation in the city when the civic government, in a round of budget cuts, decided to stop funding the swans' upkeep (the birds have to be rounded up, sheltered, and fed during the winter). After the city launched a search for sponsors, local high-tech firm Cognos Incorporated ponied up the necessary funds. The swans are usually afloat on the river between May and October. Each pair has its own nesting grounds and territory. You're never guaranteed a swan spotting, but two of the best places to look for them are **Brewer Park** (off Bronson Avenue) and **Strathcona Park** (Range Road at Somerset Avenue East).

SECRET
SWEATERS

For those who want to dress like a lady of the manor at almost peasant prices, there's **Luce's Ladies' Sweater Shop** (146 Colonnade Road South, 224-7866). Don't let the industrial strip-mall setting put you off. Even though many of the classic cotton and wool sweaters and cardigans are designed on the premises, and some of the other clothes are made in the Far East, everything has that upper-crust English feel that just screams horses and afternoon tea. For the deepest discounts, check out the off-season merchandise displayed in the small room to the left of the entrance.

SECRET
TAVERNS

They're not pubs, or eateries, or lounges, or clubs. They're taverns, where men's men (and the women who love 'em) gather to knock back large quantities of beer. There are probably a few dart boards, a pool table or two, a long, scarred bar, and a few barflies who were sitting on the same barstools when the TV behind the bar was black-and-white.

The granddaddy of Ottawa's taverns is the venerable **Chateau Lafayette** (42 York Street, 241-4747). I've always had a soft spot for the place since it supplied pretty much the only note of glamour in my otherwise squeaky-clean university career. With a group of similarly fresh-faced frosh, I acquired the dubious distinction of being booted out of the Laff for the simple crime of wearing a Carleton University sweatshirt (just a few days before we showed up, a rowdier group of our fellow students had treated the joint to a barroom brawl). When you tell people that you were once kicked out of the Laff, they suddenly regard you with newfound respect. The bar was founded in 1849, and for a long time it looked every bit its age. The eastern half of the building has been spruced up — you can even order quesadillas, for heaven's sake — but the western half is just as dim and atmospheric as ever, with a stained-glass pool lamp straight out of *The Hustler* dangling over the pool table.

Three generations of the Disipio family have been packing patrons into the **Prescott** (379 Preston Street, 232-4217, www.theprescott.com) since 1934. The sports bar serves up 60,000 of its famous quarter-pound meatball sandwiches every year. It's the place where hockey players past and present hang out; late Canadiens star Aurel Joliat, an Ottawa boy born and bred, was a regular. Boxing fans came to the Prescott to roast boxer Rocky Marciano in the 1960s, and baseball fans swing by today to raise a glass with players from the Expos or the Blue Jays passing through town on promotional tours. Race fans can also indulge in some off-track betting here.

S E C R E T
TEA

✣

The Tea Party (119 York Street, 562-0352) purveys more than 100 blends of tea and coffee. A cozy, favourite-aunt kind of spot, filled to the brim with eccentric teapots and flowered mugs, it's a great place to treat yourself to afternoon tea without breaking the bank: an English-style cream tea with scones and jam is just $4.95.

You can't enjoy the big breakfasts at the **Albert House Inn** (478 Albert Street, 236-4479) unless you're staying there overnight. But if you're a tea lover, you might want to check in: the inn offers about 60 kinds of tea in its dining room. And the inn, located in a rambling old mansion built in 1875, is a great place to soak up some Victorian atmosphere.

Tiffin Time (1255 Wellington Street, 722-4832, www.tiffintime.com) is a pleasant if somewhat schizophrenic place. It shares the sunny first floor of the building with a bookshop called **Leadmark Incorporated** (761-1177, www.leadmark.ca), where you can pick up tomes on spirituality, goal setting, and self-help topics as well as motivational tapes and mugs emblazoned with "get rich quick" messages. So, once you're all hepped up to pursue excellence and conquer the devil within, wander across the room to Tiffin Time to relax with a cup of herbal tea or Indian chai (for hopeless type A's, there are also lots of caffeinated brews).

SECRET
TEXAS

Started by former Rough Riders player and Houston native Val Belcher, the **Lone Star Café** (780 Baseline Road, 224-4044, www.lonestarcafe.com) is now an Ottawa institution that has outlasted the football team. It started as a barbecue stand at Lansdowne Park, where

Belcher served up "Belcher Burgers" during Riders home games. He opened this west-end location in May 1986 and has since expanded the chain across Ontario and into the Maritimes. But this is the original down-home dining experience. The portions are huge, the music is loud, and the place is always packed; come at lunch — early — if you want to avoid a long wait. (You can make reservations only if you have a group of eight or more, and then only at off-peak times.)

Just east of downtown, **Zuma's Texas Grill and Dance Hall** (1211 Lemieux Street, 742-9378) serves up Tex-Mex and Louisiana food in a huge, restored, board-and-batten house. You'll be able to see the bright blue gables from the Queensway. Wednesday is karaoke night, while most other evenings you can indulge in a little line dancin'.

Need appropriate garb for your night at Zuma's? Mosey on out to the west end for an extensive selection of western duds at **Texas Connection** (19 Stafford Road, Nepean, 721-3390). Here you can plow through shelves of western boots in every colour: teal, bright pink with blue hearts, purple, and more. Wrangler jeans, suede vests, elaborate denim dresses, skirts and jackets studded with silvery beads and rhinestones, belts, buckles, bolo ties, and hats — you name it, they stock it. The store hours are shorter than many others in the neighbourhood, so call ahead.

At the other end of Bells Corners, there's a smaller but still good selection of western gear at **Saddle Creek** (150 Robertson Road, Nepean, 829-3030). It sells fringed jackets, Australian outback casual wear and coats, all kinds of vests and hats, and nifty turquoise jewellery. You'll also find plenty of boots, English and western tack, and riding helmets.

SECRET
THAI

Since the early 1990s, Ottawa has become a hotbed of Thai cuisine. Lemongrass seems to waft across every second corner. I'm an extremely uncritical Thai diner, never having found a Thai restaurant in town that I didn't love. Here are some of the most popular places; all of them offer memorable meals.

With its whitewashed exterior, blue trim, and cheerful window boxes, **Siam Bistro** (1268 Wellington Street, 728-3111) looks more like a Swiss country house than a Thai restaurant. It is regularly packed with enthusiastic Westboro diners. I often get **Green Papaya** (260 Nepean Street, 231-8424) and **Coriander Thai** (282 Kent Street, 233-2828) confused since they're just a few blocks apart and serve great food; the decor at Green Papaya is a little more vivid, and the restaurant boasts a tiny verandah with four tables. I know people who drive across town to get takeout from the **Siam Kitchen** (1050 Bank Street, 730-3954), which also has sit-down dining. In Bells Corners, **Sukhothai Restaurant** (130 Robertson Road, Nepean, 829-1010) attracts devoted fans of spicy fare.

SECRET
THEATRE

The **Great Canadian Theatre Company** (910 Gladstone Avenue, 236-5196, www.gctc.ca) believes that live professional theatre shouldn't break the budget. It offers cut-rate subscriptions for students, seniors, and low-income patrons as well as at least one "pay-what-you-can" performance per run. The fare is some of the most cutting-edge theatre in Ottawa.

Two local amateur theatre companies claim different distinctions for longevity. The **Orpheus Musical Theatre Society** (17 Fairmont Avenue, 729-4318, www.orpheus-theatre.on.ca) has been operating under a variety of names since 1906. It lays claim to being North America's longest-running amateur musical theatre company. Orpheus puts on three full-scale musicals every year, from old favourites such as *A Funny Thing Happened on the Way to the Forum* to world premieres (the company has commissioned three original shows). It owns the building on Fairmont, which it uses for set building and rehearsals, but it puts on its shows at Nepean's **Centrepointe Theatre**, which you should contact for tickets (101 Centrepointe Drive, Nepean, 727-6650). Across town, meanwhile, the **Ottawa Little Theatre** (400 King Edward Avenue, 233-0197) proclaims itself to be "Canada's oldest continuing theatre." (It was founded in 1913.) It puts on eight productions each year as well as a summer musical. For years, the OLT had a reputation as a "safe" place for theatre, where undemanding regulars who'd been buying season tickets since the Pearson era could see popular, middle-of-the-road chestnuts such as *Our Town*. Lately, though, it has branched out into more challenging territory.

Every summer, the professional **Odyssey Theatre** (232-8407) puts on a *commedia dell'arte*-inspired show in Sandy Hill's Strathcona Park (Range Road at Somerset Street East). This over-the-top style of Italian farce, complete with masks and puppetry, isn't for everyone. However, if you enjoy broadly played absurdity, the location next to the Rideau River is a wonderful place to watch a play unfold under the stars. Come early and bring a picnic.

S E C R E T
TOOLS

Lee Valley Tools (1000 Morrison Drive, 596-9202, www.leevalley.com) is primarily a mail-order store. But it does have a spacious shop next to its headquarters in Ottawa's west end, where woodworkers and gardeners can browse and daydream about all sorts of arcane doodads: stainless steel and maple tools, Italian plastic garden clogs, microwave flower presses, jeweller's clamps, back-support belts, and other implements that look to my untrained eye like leftovers from a medieval torture chamber.

S E C R E T
TOYS

Mrs. Tiggy Winkle's toy store has several shopping-mall outlets around town. But my favourite location is still the two-storey shop in the Glebe (809 Bank Street, 234-3836), a bright, sunny place where you can find stuff for actual kids and kids at heart alike. There are Pez dispensers and lollipops, board games and wooden toys, T-shirts and coffee mugs, books and stuffed animals. And, for simple people like me, there are lots of no-batteries-required items, such as Slinkies, rubber balls, and skipping ropes. Bring a scythe if you plan on getting through the crowd in December.

SECRET
TRIVIA

Of course, I'm biased. But *Jeopardy*-heads and Regis Philbin-philes can get their fix of live trivia every week at a quiz night hosted by some guy named Paul Paquet, who happens to have cosigned my mortgage and marriage certificate. Head to the **Barley Mow** (1080 Bank Street, 730-1279) on Mondays.

Other nights of the week, you'll have to make do with NTN Trivia, a computerized trivia system that pits players in bars across the continent against each other. It's not bad, but it's a bit slow, giving you lots of time to order another round. A number of bars around the city have the system — the **New Edinburgh Pub** (1 Beechwood Avenue, 748-9809) claims to be the city's busiest NTN venue, with 30 remote consoles. But the keenest players whom I've stumbled across play at **Puzzles** (344 Richmond Road, 728-3024), a down-home sports bar in Westboro. Like Cheers, this is the kind of place where everyone seems to know each other; you half expect someone to yell out "Norm!" at some point in the evening. The bar has been here forever, and I suspect that some of the regulars have too.

Once a year, the **Champions for Children World Trivia Night** (745-1893, www.cfc.ottawa.com/index.html) brings almost 2,000 die-hard trivia buffs together at the Ottawa Civic Centre at Lansdowne Park for a long, fun night of pizza, beer, and tough trivia. Get together a team of 10, and register early — this fund-raising event regularly sells out.

SECRET
ULTIMATE

Ottawa is home to the largest Ultimate Frisbee league in the world. From just five teams when it began in 1986, the **Ottawa Carleton Ultimate Association** (www.ocua.ca) had ballooned to 233 teams and more than 2,600 members by 1999. The league has even purchased its own 100-acre site just south of Ottawa. Every summer, various leagues organize a mind-boggling number of games in parks across the capital region. The best place for current information is the large, well-organized web site. You can also find out about upcoming events at **CD Exchange** (142 Rideau Street, 241-9864), which also sells Ultimate equipment.

SECRET
VEGETARIAN

The peculiarly named **Satisfaction-Perfection-Promise** (167 Laurier Avenue East, 234-7299) is something of a shrine to New Age guru Sri Chinmoy: wall plaques celebrate his achievements, and his books, tapes, and CDs are on sale at the counter. Whether you subscribe to Chinmoy's philosophy or not, the food is tasty and inexpensive. The menu ranges from Thai noodle salad to vegan desserts. Don't miss the flaky vegetable samosas with cucumber dill sauce, though I haven't had the nerve to try the vegetarian poutine: a sauce of white cheese curd and mushroom gravy poured over mashed potatoes.

The Green Door (198 Main Street, 234-9597) serves up all its vegetarian dishes for the same price, $15 a kilogram. So you can chow down on a mountain of green salad for about the same price as a few sesame cookies. It's a serve-yourself buffet, and there's usually a good choice of salads, stews, vegetarian quiches, healthy breads, and desserts. Many dishes are wheat-free, dairy-free, and/or vegan, and a number of the recipes are reprinted in the restaurant's own cookbook (available at the cash register). The atmosphere is casual and friendly, and about half of the seating is at long, communal tables.

Call first before heading to **The Pantry** (Glebe Community Centre, 690 Lyon Street, 564-1058), a vegetarian tearoom tucked away in the corner of a former church. It's usually open weekdays for lunch only but only at certain times of the year. The mostly organic fare includes soups, salads, sandwiches, and baked goods.

Govinda's (212 Somerset Street East, 565-6544) is a nonsmoking, alcohol-free vegetarian restaurant run by the Hare Krishna Temple. It offers an all-you-can-eat hot-and-cold buffet at a very reasonable price (about seven dollars per person).

For fresh, pesticide-free vegetables and herbs, check out the **Ottawa Organic Farmer's Market** (Kingsway United Church, 630 Island Park Drive, 256-4150) held on Saturdays from 10 a.m. to 2 p.m.

SECRET
VICTORIANA

Ottawa has always had a soft spot for Queen Victoria since she chose the rough lumber town as a national capital. My favourite statue of her is the gothic monument between the Centre Block and the West Block on Parliament Hill. The regal pose and Latin inscription are just so . . . imperial. There's another "we are not amused" likeness of her inside the Centre Block, holding pride of place inside the magnificent **Parliamentary Library**. The library itself is a sumptuous piece of Victorian architecture, the only part of the original Centre Block that was saved when the rest of the building burned to the ground in 1916. Even if you're not remotely interested in politics, take the Centre Block tour just to see this circular room with its tiers of carved shelving and elegant domed roof.

Want a hint of Victoriana in your wedding dress? Try **Donna Kearns** (146 Dalhousie Street, 241-6369), where you can order a custom-made confection and relax during the fittings in an ambience of overstuffed boudoir chairs and long velvet drapes.

S E C R E T
VIDEOS
❀

If you're bored with the video selection at the big chains, don't despair. I guarantee that you haven't seen all of the 4,000 flicks at **The Invisible Cinema** (354-A Elgin Street, 2nd floor, 237-0769). With the slogan "films for all tastes (or lack thereof)," partners Wyatt Boyd and Pam Meldrum stock movies in categories that you'll never see at the local Blockbusters outlet, including trash, New York underground, and drugsploitation. You'll also find silents, film noir gems, cult movies, documentaries, gay/lesbian/bisexual movies, indie flicks, dance movies, and all four volumes of *Contemporary Estonian Animation*. Boyd will be happy to give you an enthusiastic tour. In many categories, the movies are shelved by director, not by title — the sure sign of a fan's paradise.

Instead of shelving films by director, **Video Mondo** (23 Beechwood Avenue, 749-6829) classifies its offbeat offerings by country. There are movies from Canada and the United States, of course, but also from Italy, Germany, France, eastern Europe, Spain, China, Japan, Australia, and many other places. There are also some new, mainstream Hollywood releases, but they tend toward the artsy or Oscar worthy. So you'd probably find *American Beauty* but not *American Pie.* There's also a selection of children's movies.

Bestsellers (Carlingwood Shopping Centre, Carling Avenue at Woodroffe Avenue, 728-0689) is probably the only video store in Ottawa that stocks opera videos. There's also a good selection of classic, rare, and offbeat flicks, including westerns, war movies, musicals, and British comedy. **Glebe Video International** (779 Bank Street, 2nd floor, 237-6252) stocks foreign and Canadian movies, American indie productions, documentaries, and classics. It's a good place to pick up a movie that made a splash at a film festival but lasted about three days in Ottawa cinemas. **Zap and Zoom Video Superstore** (1066 Somerset Street West, 725-1144) has an extensive selection of videos, including karaoke videos and about 500 foreign films.

Speaking of foreign films, numerous rental stores specialize in fare from particular countries. **Viet Hoa** (878 Somerset Street West, 234-9320) and **Dai-Nam Video** (120 Eccles Street, 234-8742) stock Asian videos, particularly Vietnamese movies. You can pick up Filipino films at the **Amy and Rose Filipino Grocery** (628 Somerset Street West, 563-0670), which also sells black tilapia, goat meat, spring-roll wrappers, and other food items. Arabic videos are available at **Video Flash** (738 Bank Street, 235-7317) and **Arabic Video Corner** (1218 Bank Street, 523-1911).

For used versions of fairly recent hits, as well as classics such as *An Affair to Remember* and *Nothing Sacred*, try **Record Centre** (1097 Wellington Street, 722-4128), where you can buy most of the videos for less than nine dollars each.

S E C R E T
VIETNAMESE

Quê Huong (947A Somerset Street West, 234-2853) is an unpretentious little restaurant on the western edge of Chinatown. Try the roll-'em-yourself spring rolls and the savory pot stickers.

I've never sat indoors at **Saigon Restaurant** (85 Clarence Street, 789-7934) even though the narrow interior is a pleasing combination of large mirrors and blue tablecloths. Get there before noon or after 2 p.m. to grab a table on the tiny sidewalk patio, and indulge in one of the Byward Market's great bargains: the lunch special of soup and three items for $7.95 (it's available from 11 a.m. to 5 p.m.). The spring rolls are crispy and hot, the beer is dewy and cold, and the staff are friendly and quick. Just about all you need in a summer lunch spot.

SECRET
VINTAGE

There's nowhere else in Ottawa quite like **Ragtime Vintage Clothing** (43 Flora Street, 233-6940). If you love old garments, you absolutely have to go there. It's almost impossible to describe the loot crammed into this 1913 building; the treats even hang from racks suspended from the pressed-tin ceiling. But here's a start: 1920s hats, psychedelic 1960s minidresses, leather jackets, hippie vests, Hawaiian shirts, platform shoes . . . you really have to visit the store to get the full effect. Ragtime also rents professionally made costumes, many purchased from costume companies' bankruptcy sales.

For used and vintage clothing, you can't beat the selection, quality, and price at **Phase 2 Clothing** (702 Bank Street, 233-1778). A friend of mine haunts the place and always comes back with amazing deals; it seems that every time I compliment her on something she's wearing she says smugly, "Phase 2!" Cotton shaker sweaters from $4.95 and a huge variety of jeans under $10 are two of the major bargains. Nostalgic men of a certain age can head to the basement to pick up a baby-blue tuxedo jacket with black piping for $19.95. For guys with more up-to-date tastes, there are racks of used but classy tuxes and morning suits upstairs. Their dates can pick through racks of evening gowns, many under $60. But the best bargains of all may be the wedding dresses in the Millennium Bridal Boutique, including a number in the unbeatable $200 to $400 price range.

SECRET
VINYL

Wander into **Get Back Records** (386 Richmond Road, 798-1468)
and browse through the haphazard shelves of LPs from the 1950s to
the 1980s; you'll probably find some bit of vinyl that sparks a long-
forgotten memory. There's a bit of everything, from jazz and folk to
rock, though the store specializes in music from the 1950s and 1960s.
But even better than the browsing is the chance to shoot the breeze
with store owner Alan Chrisman: salesman, impresario, rock band
manager, and all-round fount of information on the history of the
capital's music scene. His first love is the Beatles — he's organized
several big Beatles conventions — but he'll gladly riff as long as
you'll let him on all kinds of topics, from foreign movies to the
mentality of bureaucrats. He's not a big fan of Westboro's increasing
gentrification, but he's vowed to stay in the neighbourhood just to be
a thorn in the sides of the civic-improvement folks. "I want to be an
eyesore!" he proclaims gleefully. Listen, learn, and buy before someone snatches that rare find from under your fingertips: Chrisman, a
professed computer hater, nevertheless sells several albums on the
eBay Internet auction site, shipping them all over the world in (un-
used) pizza boxes from the Newport Restaurant down the street. If
you love music, don't miss this place.

SECRET
WATCHES

If you secretly yearn for a pocket watch just like the one that your grandfather used to have, go to **Chronos** (inside Bank Street Antiques, 1136 Bank Street, 730-0084). It also sells other kinds of small antiques, but the collection of vintage pocket and wrist watches is one of the best in the city.

Rings Etc. (137 Bank Street, 230-8280) has a decent selection of "previously enjoyed" watches; if Gucci and Cartier watches catch your fancy, you can get them here for a fraction of the original price. It's also a good place to try if your watch breaks down on the weekend; it's one of the few downtown stores that has a watch-repair technician on the premises then.

SECRET
WATERFALLS

Just south of Carleton University, on the Rideau River, is **Hogs Back Falls** (Hog's Back Road between Riverside Drive and Colonel By Drive). The odd name comes from the fact that an early settler thought they looked like the spine of a pig — an allusion that probably held more for 19th-century farmers than for modern urbanites. Despite the unromantic name, the falls are a popular destination for cyclists. However, the park is often half empty even though there's a good-sized parking lot and a small concession stand. If you're on a bike, you can cycle along a paved path from Hogs Back Falls all the way to the river's end at **Rideau Falls** (Sussex Drive; parking lot is opposite Stanley Avenue, next to the French Embassy). It's hard to tell, looking at the well-manicured park that wraps around the site today, but these falls were the industrial heart of nearby New Edinburgh in the 19th century. The entrepreneur who built Rideau Hall, now home to the governor general, made his fortune running all sorts of mills at this site.

For a smaller but less urban waterfall, head to the **Mackenzie King Estate** in Gatineau Park (Kingsmere Road, Gatineau Park, Quebec, 819-827-2020). A short trail from King's country retreat, Moorside, leads to a quietly gurgling waterfall that was one of the prime minister's favourite places to ponder the meaning of life. Most visitors to the site miss it entirely, so it's often as secluded and peaceful as King found it.

Also in Gatineau Park, a steep, two-and-a-half-hour hike along the Eardley Escarpment will bring you to **Luskville Falls**. As well as seeing the falls, you'll have a spectacular sweeping view of the Ottawa River and its valley. To get there, follow Quebec Highway 148 west from Hull to Luskville and look for the signs on your right marking the entrance to Gatineau Park. The trailhead starts in the parking lot. For detailed directions, pick up a trail map at the park office on the *other* side of the park (33 Scott Road, Chelsea, Quebec, 819-827-2020). The escarpment itself runs through the park, and several other trails give you access to it.

S E C R E T
WEATHER REPORTS

Don't waste your time waiting for The Weather Channel to give you tomorrow's forecast. Get the news right away by calling **Environment Canada**'s weather-information line at 998-3439.

S E C R E T
WEB CAMS

For a computerized view of goings-on in the capital, check out these web cams: www.ottawacitizen.com/parliament/ (Parliament Hill); webcam.engsoc.carleton.ca/ (an auditorium lobby at Carleton University); woheaven.com/WebCams/Ottawa1.htm (O'Connor Street at the Queensway, looking north); woheaven.com/WebCams/Ottawa2.htm (a view of the Queensway looking east from O'Connor); and woheaven.com/WebCams/Ottawa3.htm (a view westward from the same vantage point).

S E C R E T
WILDLIFE

For mysterious reasons, the grassy area next to the Nicholas Street ramp onto the westbound Queensway is honeycombed with groundhog holes. The fat little guys often stand on their hind legs by the shoulder of the road, so watch out.

SECRET
WINE

Vineyards Wine Bar (54 York Street, 241-4270), a smoky cellar of red-checkered tablecloths and candlelit corners in the Byward Market, offers a mind-boggling variety of wines by the glass. For a more elegant, trendy, and expensive ambience, the **Echo Café and Wine Bar** (221 Echo Drive, 234-1528) overlooking the Rideau Canal at the Pretoria Bridge has a list of about 60 wines and often hosts events of the Ottawa Sommeliers Guild. A local wine writer also runs wine-appreciation classes in a tiny upstairs room.

ACKNOWLEDGEMENTS

This book truly would not have been possible without the help of countless people who shared their love of this city with me. Many thanks to everyone who submitted ideas through the Secret Cities web site at secretcities.com or directly to me, including the following: Brenda Bélanger, Jim Bronskill, Sarah Brown, Theo Chan, Gordon Cullingham, Adele Caren Dolgin, Karen Dooner, Janis Downey, Joyce Dubuc, Teresa Eckford, Katharine Fletcher, Sylvia Haines, Amy Heron, Jackie Holden, Stu Hoover, Yvonne Jeffery Hope, Lorrie Hubbert, Heather Hurst, Susan Joyce, Hugh Kruzel, A. Lu, Madeline McBride, Anne McCotter, Wallace McLean, Dina Milne, Arthur Owen, Aliza Rudner, Stephanie Ryan, David Scrimshaw, Glen Shackleton, Hope Thexton, Marie Danielle Vachon, Michel Vachon, Andrea Wershof, and Megan Williams. In addition, I would like to thank everyone at *Ottawa City Magazine* and *Where*, both produced by Capital Publishers; the articles that I've written for both magazines over the years have provided the basis for many a "secret" in this book. My hat is off to Claire Hooker, who checked every phone number listed. Finally, I offer my boundless gratitude to my husband, Paul Paquet, who kept me going when I was terrified that I would be buried alive in a mountain of notes and half-finished paragraphs. This one's for you.

THE SECRET FUTURE

No tour guide can be definitively comprehensive, especially when the aim is to uncover those hidden places that have previously escaped notice. Undoubtedly, some worthwhile attractions have remained hidden even from our best efforts to ferret them out.

In the interest of our own self-improvement, we ask readers to let us know of the places they've unearthed that they believe warrant inclusion in future editions of *Secret Ottawa*. If we use your suggestion, we'll send you a free copy on publication. Please contact us at the following address:

Secret Ottawa
c/o ECW PRESS

2120 Queen Street East, Suite 200
Toronto, Ontario, Canada M4E 1E2

Or e-mail us at: ecw@sympatico.ca

PHOTO SITES

SUBJECT INDEX

ALPHABETICAL INDEX